ENTERTAINING

Emily Post's

ENTERTAINING

A CLASSIC GUIDE TO ADDING ELEGANCE
AND EASE TO ANY FESTIVE OCCASION

PEGGY POST

HarperPerennial
A Division of HarperCollinsPublishers

EMILY POST'S® ENTERTAINING. Copyright © 1998 by Emily Post Institute, Inc.
All rights reserved. Printed in the United States of America. No part of this book may
be used or reproduced in any manner whatsoever without written permission except
in the case of brief quotations embodied in critical articles and reviews.
For information address HarperCollins Publishers Inc.,
10 East 53rd Street, New York, NY 10022.

HarperCollins books may be purchased for educational, business, or
sales promotional use. For information please write:
Special Markets Department, HarperCollins Publishers Inc.,
10 East 53rd Street, New York, NY 10022.

FIRST EDITION

ILLUSTRATIONS © LAURA HARTMAN MAESTRO

DESIGNED BY BTD / BETH TONDREAU

LIBRARY OF CONGRESS CATALOGING-IN-PUBLICATION DATA

Post, Peggy, 1945–
    Emily Post's entertaining: a classic guide to adding elegance and
    ease to any festive occasion / by Peggy Post.—1st ed.
          p.   cm.
    ISBN 0-06-273640-X
    1. Entertaining.   I. Title.
    BJ2021. P68 1998   98–7309
    395.3—dc21   CIP

98 99 00 01 02 ❖/RRD 10 9 8 7 6 5 4 3 2 1

CONTENTS

INTRODUCTION

"Etiquette is the foundation upon which social structure is built. Every human contact is made smooth by etiquette, or awkward by lack of it."

—EMILY POST, 1928

In an interview in *The American Weekly* in 1949, a reporter asked Emily Post her opinion of a statement she had written nearly 30 years earlier in the landmark best-seller *Etiquette: The Blue Book of Social Usage.* It concerned the issue of a young woman traveling without a chaperone. "A young girl unprotected by a chaperone," wrote Mrs. Post, "is in the position of an unarmed traveler alone among wolves."

Over 30 years later, what did the new, modernized Emily Post think of her own advice? Preposterous, she said. "Imagine me writing anything like that! The world was different then, wasn't it?"

My great-grandmother-in-law understood that the rules of social etiquette are flexible. She once said that manners are like primary colors, employing guidelines that one adapts or tailors to meet new or changing situations. Good manners, she said, were nothing more complicated than consideration for other people, a sensitive awareness to the needs of others. As a seasoned guest and hostess of all manner of celebratory occasions, Emily Post didn't blink when a fork was misplaced or a wineglass was the wrong size; to her, what was unforgivable on the part of a host or hostess was neglecting to "do what is comfortable both for those around you and for yourself." That, she said, is good manners—nothing more, nothing less.

I couldn't agree more. The cardinal principle of etiquette is thoughtfulness, and the guiding rule of thoughtful entertaining is the Golden Rule: Do unto others as you would have them do unto you. After all, the prime objective as a host or hostess is to make one's guests feel comfortable and welcome, not hold them hostage to a rigid set of tedious rules. The hosts are there to smooth any anxious wrinkles and infect the occasion with the spirit of hospitality and generosity.

The best hosts spin magic out of thin air, creating the kind of special occasion guests can't stop talking about. Who can forget that wonderful dinner party where you first tasted fresh oysters and sipped vintage champagne as you enjoyed warm conversation with old friends and new acquaintances? Who can forget the excitement of getting ready for an elegant affair, anticipating a night filled with possibility? Social occasions are filled with many such grand memories, such as:

- The ski weekend when you and your party drank hot buttered rum and warmed to a roaring fire in the lodge after a glorious day of skiing.
- The Holiday Open House, where the smell of evergreen, the glittering lights, and warm greetings from friends embodied the spirit of the season.
- The campfire when you and your friends roasted especially tasty fare under a starlit sky on an Indian-summer night.
- The last-minute party for a big promotion, where guests dined on Chinese takeout and paper plates and ended up dancing barefoot to big-band tunes in the living room.

These wonderful times with friends and loved ones remind us that we are all a part of a larger whole. Whether you're entertaining friends, business associates, or new acquaintances, open up home and hearth and surround your guests in warmth and good cheer. The reward is often an unforgettably fine occasion, one indelibly etched in the hearts of all involved.

Peggy Post
October 1998

I. PREPARING FOR A FINE OCCASION

"The proper selection of guests is the first essential in all entertaining. Taste in house furnishings or in clothes or in selecting a cook is as nothing compared to taste in people! . . . Choose your guests exactly as an artist combines flowers in a bouquet; the greater the artist, the greater the variety he can combine."

—EMILY POST, *Etiquette* (1922)

CHAPTER 1

SIZING UP THE CELEBRATION

How does a good host or hostess ensure that a good time is had by all? Entertaining is a joy when you keep the following in mind.

- **REMAIN CALM** Entertaining doesn't have to be a monumental undertaking, taking on the proportions of a crisis. Simplicity is often the best approach. Get help if necessary. Never let your guests think you're huffing and puffing: panic is contagious.
- **BE PRACTICAL** Emily Post advised a "pragmatic approach"—everything she did was geared to commonsense practicality. She even designed a movable tea tray, a device to make tea serving simpler.
- **WORK WITHIN YOUR BUDGET** Be realistic. Cut back on the size of your guest list if necessary. You don't have to buy luxury foods or wines or prepare a fancy, complicated dish to have a successful party.
- **STICK WITH WHAT YOU KNOW** Don't experiment on your guests; in other words, don't serve something you haven't made before or plot an elaborate evening you're ill-equipped to handle.

A MATTER OF SPACE

As you assess the space you have available for entertaining, it is important to decide on the degree of formality you want and can achieve within that space. Someone who lives in a small house with a large deck or patio would most likely be more comfortable inviting several guests to a barbecue or backyard picnic than to a formal dinner, while someone who has rooms with generous proportions could more easily give a formal dinner party.

Another consideration: basic supplies. Do you have enough chairs, place settings, glasses, and the necessary pots and pans to accommodate the number of invited guests? If your party is large and you are having it in a big space other than your home—say, in a reception hall—you may want to enlist the help of a party-planning service or party-rental company, which will rent almost any kind of party supply, from chairs to coat racks to china to linens. Even if your party is at home, and you have the necessary items, you may consider renting supplies if you don't want to worry about using your own or you prefer to use matching place settings.

If your living space is limited, you can become adept at working with it. In a small apartment, the party meal can be served directly from the stove, buffet-style; one-pot meals might even become a host's specialty. Arranging the space so that guests are able to move about comfortably can be the trickiest aspect of entertaining in a small space. The answer to that problem may be breaking up the room. Arranging the furniture into several intimate clusters can result in cozy conversational areas. The creation of small clusters works equally well in large spaces, where if you don't break up the space it can seem isolating and empty. Either way, by arranging the furniture into intimate clusters, you'll create a festive atmosphere humming with little pockets of chatter.

Consider as well having fold-up furniture that can stretch your dining accommodations. Card tables are very useful and can easily be tucked away in a closet until their next use. Tabletops placed on top of a smaller table and covered with a pretty tablecloth can be used to add space to a table—whether leaves that can expand your existing dining-room table, collapsible tabletops, or simply large square or round tops that can be stored standing up in a closet. Make sure, however, that when the tabletop is in place it is solid and sturdy.

Whether you are planning a dinner party, a cocktail affair, or a Super Bowl chili party, keep your guests' comfort foremost in your thoughts. If you want to have a seated dinner, you'll need a very large dinner table, or you can place smaller tables around. For many hosts and hostesses, the latter choice is a favorite way to serve dinner; it feels much cozier and encourages relaxed, intimate groups.

THE GUEST LIST
NUMBER OF GUESTS

After first deciphering how many guests your space can hold, the type of party you're going to throw can determine how many guests to invite and whether you intend to have help in serving food. In these casual times—and with the help of modern conveniences and easier access to a variety of foods—there is no set rule for the number of dinner guests you can comfortably serve yourself. It used to be that eight people was the maximum number you could serve by yourself at a sit-down dinner. You can certainly cook for as many guests as you want, but to serve a seated dinner of more than eight efficiently and quickly, you may want to either change a sit-down dinner to a buffet or enlist a friend to help you serve. For more than 16, you may need two friends or temporary help. You'll need someone to help serve drinks, pass hors d'oeuvres, serve dinner, and clean up in the kitchen. Greater numbers generally require more help.

A CONGENIAL MIX

The most venerated hosts and hostesses agree that the right mix of people—the most "congenial stew"—can make all the difference in concocting a successful party. You might enjoy mixing and matching people who don't know one another but who you believe will get on famously.

Your primary requisite is to invite guests who are likely to be interesting to one another. Additionally, it is wise to include guests upon whom you can count to be sensitive, thoughtful, and entertaining so that your concern for drawing out those who may be quiet or shy is not a burden on you alone. When seating your guests, remember their likes and dislikes: avoid seating two people next to each other who are on extreme opposite sides of a touchy, controversial issue.

A guest list composed of equal numbers of men and women is not necessary, although an "all couples and one single" party may make the one single uncomfortable. It is better to also invite a few single women and men so that no one feels like an unescorted extra, unless your dinner party is made up of very close friends who all are comfortable being together whether they are part of a pair or going solo.

CHAPTER 2

INVITATIONS

There is little so heartwarming as going to the mailbox and finding an attractive invitation from a friend for a get-together. It's fun, it's flattering—someone is taking the time and trouble to entertain and wants you to be part of the celebration. Invitations can be anything from a spontaneous same-day phone call ("We're celebrating Jack's new job and hope you and Bill are free at six for a barbecue!") to a formal invitation to a wedding sent four to six weeks in advance. The first invitation is made in person or by telephone, while the second can be elegantly printed and mailed. Both have guidelines, and both require immediate replies.

TIMING

Whether you're mailing out printed invitations or phoning guests, timing is key. Issuing an invitation at the right time allows invitees plenty of time to respond and gives you breathing room to tally the guest list and make your preparations. The concern, for most people, is to get invitations out early. Sometimes, however, even that can backfire.

A friend, Mary, was having lunch with another friend, Sue, who mentioned that she was having a party two months hence. "Be sure to put it on your calendar!" were Sue's last words to Mary at lunch. On the date of the party— no Mary. An advance invitation of two months proved too early, and Mary simply forgot to mark her calendar. So the motto is: You can be too late, but you can also be too early!

The following are general guidelines for timing your invitations to avoid sending them out too late or too early. Keep in mind that these guidelines are estimates and are not set in stone; timing may vary according to your particular circumstances, regional customs, and preferences.

WHEN DO THE INVITATIONS GO OUT?

FORMAL DINNER	3 TO 6 WEEKS
INFORMAL DINNER	FROM A FEW DAYS AWAY TO 3 WEEKS
COCKTAIL PARTY	2 TO 4 WEEKS
ANNIVERSARY PARTY	3 TO 6 WEEKS
THANKSGIVING DINNER	2 WEEKS TO 2 MONTHS
CHRISTMAS PARTY	1 MONTH
BAR MITZVAH	1 MONTH
GRADUATION PARTY	3 WEEKS
BON VOYAGE PARTY	LAST MINUTE TO 3 WEEKS
HOUSEWARMING PARTY	FROM A FEW DAYS TO 3 WEEKS
LUNCH OR TEA	FROM A FEW DAYS TO 2 WEEKS

INVITATIONS BY TELEPHONE

When inviting close friends to an informal dinner, barbecue, or small gathering for cocktails or dessert and coffee, a telephone invitation is perfectly acceptable. What you want to avoid however, when calling to extend your invitation is saying, "Hi, Mary. What are you doing Saturday night?" or "Are you busy tonight at six?" This maneuver puts Mary in an embarrassing spot. If she answers, "nothing," she is left with little choice but to accept the invitation to dine with the Borings, do a favor, baby-sit for children, or help out in other ways. On the other hand, if Mary answers, "I have plans" and then is told that she would have been invited to something she likes very much, she will be disappointed. A person who says she is busy and is then told, "Too bad you can't come, because Mr. Brilliant was looking forward to meeting you," cannot change her mind and say, "Oh, then I'll get out of my dinner somehow and come." To do so would be rude to everyone concerned.

Whenever issuing a telephone invitation, start right out with the facts: "Hi, Mary, we're having a few people on Saturday night for dinner. Can you join us?" Mary is then free to accept or decline.

In responding to a telephone invitation, it is rude to say, "I'll let you know," unless it is immediately followed by an explanation such as "I'll have to ask John if he has made any commitments for that weekend" or "We have tickets for the high-school play for that night, but perhaps I can exchange them for

Invitations

two on Friday." Without this sort of explanation, "I'll let you know" sounds as though you are simply waiting for a better invitation to come along. You should get back to the caller as soon as possible—no longer than one day—with your response.

WRITTEN INVITATIONS

When the event is of a more formal nature or is planned to honor a special guest or to celebrate a particular event, the invitation is preferably sent by mail. Like any other type of correspondence, the form and content of the written invitation is a reflection of the sender, so take care to select invitations that convey the proper formality or mood of the event.

When invitations are sent out, *every* guest should receive one. This is not the place to save expenses by verbally inviting good friends and neighbors when invitations have been mailed to everyone else. Should the good friends and neighbors find out that others received a more formal invitation, they will feel as though they were last-minute, fill-in invitees, not on your original list of guests. In addition, best friends should reply in the same manner as everyone else when they receive an invitation.

ELECTRONIC INVITATIONS

The use of e-mail to convey messages has become as commonplace as calling on the telephone. In fact, that is exactly the way e-mail should be used when issuing invitations as a replacement for the kind of casual invitation you would make by phone. E-mail invitations should be sent for casual, informal get-togethers only; they should not be sent for fancy formal parties or weddings.

If you are hooked up to the Internet, take advantage of the many Web sites that offer a variety of invitation "cards" that you can personalize, print out, and send in the mail or quickly e-mail.

If you want to make sure a guest received an e-mail, simply send your message with a return receipt, which lets you know if and when the message has been opened.

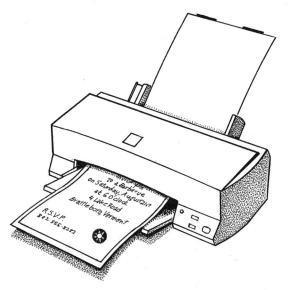

THE RANGE OF INVITATIONS

For invitations to informal dinners or parties, the attractive, decorated, preprinted ones available at stationery and card stores are perfectly acceptable and practical. Extremely casual invitations can be written on notepaper or an informal note or extended by telephone or e-mail. For very formal dinners, invitations may be engraved or written by hand in the third-person style.

INFORMAL INVITATIONS

For informal occasions, the attractively designed and decorated fill-in invitations sold for every sort of entertainment are widely used. Many of these are charming and in the best of taste. Some can be personalized via computer in your local stationery store; others are offered on the Internet. The telephone is also a perfectly acceptable means of extending an informal invitation; just be clear about the date and hour—and leave your guests in no doubt about what is intended. For informal gatherings, it is up to you as host to decide whether to send written invitations or telephone your friends to ask them to join you.

The use of informals (small fold-over notepapers) for invitations is acceptable. If the informal is mono-grammed or unmarked, the invitation takes the form of a brief note and must

YOU ARE INVITED
FOR COCKTAILS

ON_____
AT_____
BY_____
RSVP_____

Invitations

include your name, since the recipient may not know who sent it. If the note is going to a close friend, the signature need be only the first name; but if there should be any question whether the receiver knows from which "Lucy" the invitation came, it is safer to include the last name.

"Third-Person" Formal Invitations for Fancy Occasions

> *Mr. and Mrs. John Senning*
> *request the pleasure of your company*
> *for dinner and dancing*
> *on Saturday, the tenth of April*
> *at half past seven o'clock*
> *Delaware Lake*
> *Delaware, Ohio*
>
> *R.S.V.P.*   *Black tie*
> *250 Garden Circle*
> *Delaware, Ohio*

Formal invitations are often engraved on white or cream cards—either plain or bordered by plate-mark (a raised border in the paper). Thermography is a relatively inexpensive printing process that simulates engraving and may be used in its place. Ask your printer to show you samples of both.

The lettering is a matter of personal choice, but keep in mind that the plainer the design, the clearer the message. Punctuation is used only when words requiring separation occur on the same line, and in certain abbreviations, such as "Mr." or "R.S.V.P."

Traditionally, the terms "black tie" or "white tie" were never used on invitations to weddings or private parties. It was assumed that people receiving formal invitations to these events would know what to wear. Today, however, the vast majority of parties are *not* formal, so the hosts who want their guests to dress formally usually must indicate this on their invitations. If the phrase "black tie" is used, it should appear in the lower right-hand corner of invitations to proms, charity balls, formal dinners or dances, evening weddings, or any event to which a wide assortment of people is invited.

Handwritten Formal Invitations and Replies

When a formal invitation to dinner or luncheon is handwritten instead of engraved, plain white or cream notepaper or paper engraved or printed with the house address or the family's crest is often used. The wording and spacing must follow the engraved model's exactly. The invitation must be written by hand—it should not be typewritten.

If the return address on the envelope is not the same as the one to which the replies are to be sent, the address for replies must be written under the R.S.V.P. in the left-hand corner of the invitation.

Replies are addressed to the person, or persons, who issues the invitation. When a response card is sent with the invitation, it should be used for the reply, rather than a handwritten response.

FORMAL DINNER INVITATIONS

Private dinners that are formal enough to demand a third-person invitation are rare, but they take place occasionally. Many diplomatic and official dinners require formal invitations. Invitations to a buffet differ from invitations to more formal dinners in that they are almost never in the formal, third-person style. They may be written on informals, notepaper, or commercial fill-in invitations.

INVITATIONS TO LUNCH

The word "luncheon" is used less these days, having been largely replaced by the more informal "lunch." Although invitations to lunch are often telephoned, an engraved card is occasionally used for an elaborate luncheon party, especially for one given in honor of someone. However, a formal invitation to lunch is more often in the form of a personal note or on a fill-in invitation. It is usually mailed at least two weeks in advance. The personal invitation might read:

Dear Gloria and John,
 Please join us for a lunch party at our home on Saturday, June 10, at 12:30 P.M. to meet Jane's fiancé, Bob Thomas.
 I do hope you will be able to join us.
    Best,
     Elaine

If the occasion is a very large lunch for which an engraved card is used, "To meet Congresswoman Lowey" should be written across the top.

INVITATION ENCLOSURES

You may need to include in your invitations other pieces of information for the guest. Enclosures are placed in front of the invitation, which is inserted with the writing facing the flap side of the envelope, so that the recipient sees the writing on the invitation and any enclosures as the invitation is removed.

- MAPS If your home, your club, or the location of the party is unfamiliar to some guests or difficult to find, it is enormously helpful and courteous to draw a map of the best route to take. Or you can write directions. Have the map or instructions reproduced, and enclose them with your invitations.

- SCHEDULE OF EVENTS This may be used when the weekend of a big wedding or event has multiple gatherings, at different venues. Directions to the events are especially valuable to out-of-town guests.

- TICKETS When the invitation is to an event where tickets are required, such as a commencement, these tickets may be enclosed with the invitation if you know the recipient will be coming and the invitation is a formality.

- RAFFLE TICKETS Charity and fund-raising organizations often enclose raffle tickets with their invitations, hoping that even if the recipient cannot attend the event, he will purchase a raffle ticket and support the organization in that way.

- RESPONSE CARDS If you have chosen to send your guests response cards for their use in replying, the card and your self-addressed stamped envelope are enclosed in front of the invitation.

REPLIES AND REGRETS

R.S.V.P.s

R.S.V.P.s seem to have become a problem for many hosts. The term "R.S.V.P."
is from the French phrase *répondez s'il vous plaît.* R.S.V.P. means "please reply"
and is often included on invitations. Unfortunately, it can't be universally
assumed that people know what the letters R.S.V.P. mean. Many hosts say that
potential guests are negligent about responding. Some hosts try to sidestep the
problem by putting "Regrets only" on an invitation, but that too often elicits
few responses. If someone doesn't respond to an R.S.V.P. and time is running
out, it's perfectly fine to call for an answer. If you have friends who have trouble
committing to something until the last minute, call them and give them a dead-
line ("We need to know by. . . "). That usually does the trick. In business entertaining, the problem is even worse. A business associate who does not respond
to an R.S.V.P. not only comes across as rude, but unprofessional as well.

To reiterate: Anyone receiving an invitation with an R.S.V.P. included is
obliged to reply as promptly as possible. It is inexcusably rude to leave someone
who has asked if you can attend a party with no idea of how many people to
expect.

How do you reply? Simply match the invitation. On most occasions—for
acceptances and when there is nothing special to say—the reply-in-kind rule
holds. A formal, third-person invitation requires a third-person reply. If you are
a close friend who wishes to explain your refusal or to express your delight in
the invitation, however, you may always write a personal note. When the
R.S.V.P. is followed by a telephone number, do your best to promptly telephone
your answer. If you can't get through to the host after several attempts, don't
give up. Leave a message, if you can, or even send a brief note saying "We'll be
there" or "So sorry, can't make it." Address your reply to the person who
issued the invitation, unless you have been asked to reply to someone else.

If the invitation says "Regrets only," don't send or call an acceptance
unless you have something to discuss with the hostess. If there is no R.S.V.P. at
all, you are not obligated to reply, but it is never wrong to do so. Any hostess
will appreciate your effort.

Sometimes an immediate "Yes" is impossible because of tentative conflicts.
If the gathering to which you have been invited is informal and you know the
hosts well, feel free to phone and explain: "I'd love to be there, but I may have

to go to Chicago. Can I let you know in a day or two?" If, however, the party is a formal one and your delayed reply affects the host's well-laid plans, then you owe it to him to decline the invitation at the start: "I hate to miss the evening, but I may have to be in Chicago. Thank you so much for including me in the invitation."

REFUSING AN INVITATION

You are not, except according to your own conscience, obligated to accept an invitation. Nor do you need to give a reason for not accepting it. In fact, if you are declining simply because you don't want to go but have no other plans, it is best not to give a reason if asked, other than "I'm terribly sorry, I'm busy that evening." This leaves you free to accept another invitation. If you make up an excuse, such as an out-of-town trip, you should not accept another invitation, or you risk hurting the feelings of those who invited you first.

If you are genuinely unable to accept an invitation from a good friend and feel that a formal, third-person reply is too distant, write a personal note instead. Once having accepted an invitation, however, you are obliged to go. You can change an acceptance to a regret only in the event of a dire emergency such as illness, a death in the family, or a sudden unavoidable trip.

Avoid being duplicitous. If you refuse an invitation using illness, a death in the family, or a sudden trip as an excuse, you must not accept another, more desirable one for the same day. For example, perhaps you have refused a cocktail party because you said you will be out of town. Then, on the night of the party you miraculously show up at another party attended by a mutual friend. You can bet that the senders of the first invitation will hear about it—and be upset. If you don't want to attend a party, use no excuse beyond "I'm afraid we are busy that evening," which leaves you free to accept something else that might come along.

ASKING FOR AN INVITATION

You should never ask for an invitation for yourself. Nor should you ask to bring an extra person to a meal or a party. When regretting an invitation you can always explain that you are expecting a weekend guest, leaving it up to the hostess-to-be to invite your guest or not. The hostess has every right to refuse to do so. But if she is having a big buffet or a large cocktail party she may not mind—and may even welcome—you bringing a houseguest.

CHANGING YOUR ANSWER

From "Yes" to "No." If a *real* emergency arises, and you find you cannot attend a function for which you have already accepted, let the hostess know immediately. If the occasion is a seated dinner or a bridge party you'll need to do so at once, since the hostess will have to find a replacement right away. If the event is a large catered party, it is also important to let your hostess know of your change of plans immediately, because caterers generally charge for the number of guests expected and not for how many actually arrive. In the case of an open house or a big cocktail party, your cancellation is not so much a practical concern as it is one of common courtesy.

In most cases a telephone call is best; it's quick and gives you a chance to explain your problem and express your regrets in person. If you prefer, however, and if there is ample time, you may write a short note giving your reason and your apologies. If the affair is a formal one or a sit-down dinner, it is then perfectly all right for the hostess to ask a close friend to fill in. It should be a friend who would be flattered, not insulted, that the hostess feels comfortable asking for last-minute help.

From "No" to "Yes." If you refuse an invitation for perfectly legitimate reasons and then find that circumstances have changed and you can attend after all, you may sometimes rescind your regrets. It all depends on the nature of the occasion. If the affair is a party of limited number, such as for a seated dinner, your spot has likely been filled. It would only embarrass the host if you ask to be reinstated. If, however, the party is a large reception, a cocktail buffet, a picnic, or any affair at which the addition of another guest or two will not likely cause any complications, you may call the host, explain your situation, and ask if you may change your regret to an acceptance.

THE OBLIGATIONS CREATED BY AN INVITATION

Parties held in someone's home, whether lunches, brunches, or cocktail and dinner parties, *do* require that you invite the host to *your* party at a later date. Wedding and shower invitations, invitations to dances, and invitations to any official function or one that you pay to attend carry no return obligations.

The payback invitation does not necessarily have to be in kind. A newly married young couple living in a tiny apartment may not have the means to invite their friends to the same kind of dinner party their friends had. The young couple must repay, however, in some way, whether by inviting their friends to lunch at their favorite deli, perhaps, or by including them in a picnic. If you receive an invitation to a large cocktail party, the next time you entertain in a similar way your cocktail-party host and hostess should be on your list. To be invited to a small dinner party is another matter. This invitation is more personal, more flattering, and should be returned in kind within a couple of months. The same is true of a weekend-visit invitation. Often it cannot be repaid at once, but when circumstances permit, you should invite your host and hostess to visit you. If you have no facilities to repay their hospitality in that way, treat them to dinner, the theater, or any entertainment you think they would especially enjoy. Wedding invitations, however, should never be used to pay back social obligations.

One attempt to return the invitation after a dinner party is not enough. If your hosts refuse your first invitation, try at least once, and preferably twice, more. After that, put the invitation on hold until some future date.

Even when you decline an invitation to a party, you incur a (milder) obligation to return the favor. The *intent* of the invitation was to entertain you and should be acknowledged by a return invitation in the not-too-distant future.

THE PROBLEM WITH PAYBACK PARTIES

People who have been invited to a great many parties and haven't the time or the energy to give a number of small parties sometimes repay their obligations by inviting everyone at once to whom they are indebted. The problems here are these: The guests are not usually chosen for compatibility; often there are not enough places to sit down; the crowd is so large that no one can move freely from group to group (or table, or bar); and the noise level reaches a deafening pitch. If you are a popular guest and incur social obligations with any frequency, try to make the effort to give small parties from time to time and avoid the necessity of a giant yearly payback.

PARTY WEAR

The rule of thumb in party wear? When in doubt, it is better to dress down (slightly) than up. Or, better yet, do some checking. Ask your hosts, or another guest, to clarify the type of clothing and degree of formality for the upcoming occasion. Dress-code suggestions do get confusing. Some of the descriptions are vague, and regions of the country have variations in customs. It's usually traditional, for example, to remove your gloves whenever you are introduced to someone indoors. When introduced to someone outdoors on a cold Minnesota day, however, you do the practical commonsense thing: Keep those gloves on.

WHAT TO WEAR?

People are often confused as to what it means when an invitation specifies a certain type of dress, from "dressy casual" and "business casual" to "white tie," "black tie," "formal," "semiformal," and "informal."

- INFORMAL OR COME CASUAL means just that: something informal and comfortable but neat, pressed, and clean. Your attire should fit the custom of the area and occasion; for a poolside party, jeans and a T-shirt, plus your bathing suit, would usually be fine. The terms "dressy casual" and "business casual"—while confusing—are becoming more prevalent. "Dressy casual" may seem a bit of a contradiction in terms; however, in these relaxed times, it may keep people from showing up in a T-shirt and torn cutoffs. For a "dressy casual" affair, wear something nicer than ordinary everyday casual clothes but not as fancy as cocktail wear. "Business casual" usually means wearing something a little more casual than customary office attire, such as khakis, sports shirts, and blazers or sweaters.
- SEMIFORMAL generally means that women wear dresses or dressy pants ensembles. Men wear either suits and ties or sports shirts, a sports jacket, a tie, and slacks. If in doubt, it is perfectly acceptable for you to check with your hostess.
- BLACK TIE OR FORMAL means men should wear tuxedos with a soft shirt and bow tie. Jackets may be white in the summer and black the rest of the year, and are available in patterns and many other colors. Women either wear long dresses, or a short, cocktail-length dress, depending upon what is currently customary in their area and for the occasion.
- WHITE TIE is the most formal evening wear—white tie, wing collar, and tailcoat. This is almost never required today, except for official and diplomatic occasions and the rare private ball. For a woman, "white tie" indicates that a long gown should be worn.

"NO SMOKING" ON INVITATIONS

Q. *What do I do if I don't want people to smoke in my house at all? Should I indicate this on the invitation?*

A. The absence of ashtrays is an excellent hint that you don't wish people to smoke. You should not write "No smoking" on the invitation, nor should you post "Thank you for not smoking" signs in your house. When guests are present who do smoke, show them where they may go outside to smoke. If you live in an apartment where there is no outside, then smokers will just have to wait until they leave. Should someone actually light a cigarette in the house, it is appropriate for you to quitely say, "I'm so sorry, John, but we don't smoke in the house. Feel free to go out on the deck whenever you want a cigarette."

CHAPTER 3

SETTING THE TABLE

A beautifully set table contributes as much to the desirability of a meal as tempting aromas wafting from the kitchen. The inspired host can create magic with color, texture, romantic lighting, the gleam of polished silverware, and the shimmer of glass and crystal. Correctly placed items facilitate the process from start to finish.

Even Emily Post sometimes needed advice on table settings. Not long after she published *Etiquette* in 1922, she found herself unclear on how to answer a reader's question on table settings. Mrs. Post decided to visit Tiffany's famed china and silver department for advice. So where did Tiffany's turn to for help? To Mrs. Post's own *Etiquette*, which the salesclerk pulled out from under Tiffany's counter and proceeded to thumb through—directly under Emily's nose.

From then on, Emily Post decided that in the absence of a clear-cut, obvious, traditional answer, she would rely instead on simple common sense to solve knotty etiquette dilemmas. The same holds true today.

FOR INFORMAL OCCASIONS

Most of us have little need these days for 10-course place settings. The American way is toward a more casual approach. Whether you call your dinner party "informal," "semiformal," or "casual," you have much more latitude in planning your table setting than you do for a formal dinner. Still, there are a few overall factors that should be given attention within the framework of your available space, your budget, the style of your home, your party's theme, and the tastes of your guests. Outside of those limitations, you should give your imagination and creativity free rein in setting a fine table.

"Informal" doesn't mean sloppy; just as with more formal settings, you'll want the settings on the table neatly and evenly spaced. The main difference between the formal and informal place setting is that the latter requires less of everything. Fewer courses are served, so fewer pieces of silver and plates are set out.

Many people like to mix and match china for striking or offbeat effects. If you do, it's a good idea to use china that shares a similar color or pattern scheme or has one piece in common throughout that is the linking design element. The same goes for the rest of the items on your informal table. You may use any material that appeals to you. Wooden salt shakers and pepper grinders, pewter plates, wooden salad bowls, ironware, pottery, and stainless-steel flatware are all fine. Again, the only rule is that each item be in keeping with the others. Don't combine plastic wineglasses with fine bone china, for example, or plastic plates with delicate crystal glasses. The secret is not in having everything of one design, but in creating, out of a variety of patterns and colors, a harmonious whole.

If you prefer to use matching china but don't have a complete set, one solution is to fill the gaps with glass. If, for example, you have no butter plates

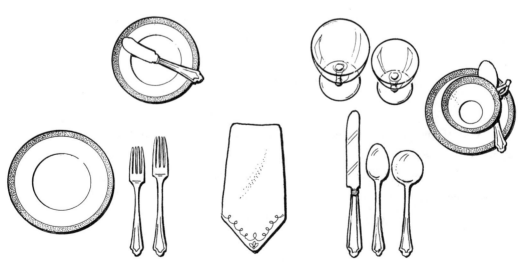

or bowls that match your china, glass plates and bowls are beautiful complements.

Plan your place setting around your menu. If you serve bread and butter, try to include a butter plate in the place setting. Serve separate salad plates if your menu includes any dishes with gravy. Salad may be put on the same plate with broiled steak, chops, or chicken, but can be an unappetizing mess when combined with chicken gravy or lamb stew.

Generally, only one or two wines are served, so a water goblet and one or two wineglasses are all that are necessary. In the event that wine is not served, iced-tea glasses are often put out.

The typical place setting for an informal three-course dinner would include the following. Notice that the silver to be used last is next to the plate.

- **TWO FORKS** One for salad at the far left and one for dinner to the left of the plate (Note: It is also correct to place the salad fork just to the left of the plate if the salad is to be served after the entrée.)
- **DINNER PLATE** Not on the table when guests sit down
- **SALAD PLATE** To the left of the forks
- **ONE DINNER KNIFE** Next to the plate on the right. For steak, chops, chicken, or game, you may use a steak knife instead.
- **TWO SPOONS** Dessert spoon to the right of the knife and soup spoon at the far right.
- **ONE BUTTER PLATE WITH BUTTER KNIFE**, if you have them
- **ONE WATER GOBLET** or tall tumbler
- **ONE WINEGLASS** if you plan to serve wine
- **NAPKIN** in the center of the place setting, or to the left of the forks

If you plan to serve coffee with the meal, the cup and saucer go to the right of the setting, with the coffee spoon on the right side of the saucer.

Service plates are not used at an informal dinner, except under soup bowls and under the stemmed glass used for shrimp cocktail and fruit cocktail. It may be a true service plate, or it may be simply another dinner or dessert plate—whichever size and style is most appropriate.

The dessert spoon and fork need not be beside the dinner plate at the start of the meal. The dessert spoon—and dessert fork, if one is to be used—can be brought in, as at a formal dinner, with the dessert plate. Or, they can be placed, American style, above the center of the place setting, horizontally, with the bowl of the spoon facing left and the tines of the fork facing right.

When your guests arrive at the table, butter should already be on the butter plates, water glasses filled, and the wine (if being served) ready to be poured. Salad is often served with the main course instead of as a separate course. In restaurants, salad is usually served before the main course in less formal restaurants. Either dress the salad before serving, or let each person add dressing to suit his or her taste.

If the host is serving the meat and vegetables, the stack of plates may be placed in front of him along with the foods to be served and the necessary implements. If there is a first course already on the table, however, the hostess or help should bring the entrée in from the kitchen after the plates have been removed.

Have any course to be served before the entrée on the table when the guests come in to dinner. Long-stemmed glass bowls containing fish or shrimp should have a plate under them. Both should be removed to make way for the main course.

THE FORMAL TABLE SETTING

The one rule for a formal table is that everything should be geometrically spaced: the centerpiece in the actual center, the place settings at equal distances, and utensils balanced. Beyond this one rule you can vary your arrangement and decorations to a wide degree. A formal place setting generally consists of the following.

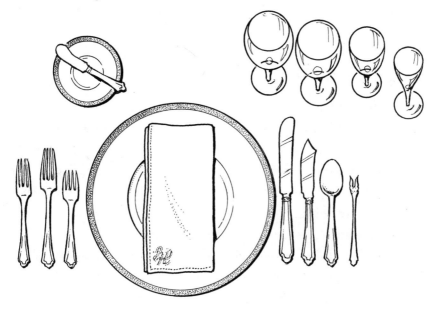

- **SERVICE PLATE** positioned so the pattern "picture" faces the diner
- **BUTTER PLATE** placed above the forks at the left of the place setting
- **WINEGLASSES** positioned according to size
- **SALAD FORK** placed directly to the left of the plate
- **MEAT FORK** positioned to the left of the salad fork
- **FISH FORK** positioned to the left of the meat fork; since it is used first, it is to the outside left
- **SALAD KNIFE** just to the right of the plate
- **MEAT KNIFE** placed to the right of the salad knife
- **FISH KNIFE** positioned to the right of the meat knife
- **BUTTER KNIFE** positioned diagonally at the top of the butter plate
- **SOUP SPOON AND/OR FRUIT SPOON** placed outside the knives
- **OYSTER FORK** if shellfish is to be served, beyond the spoons; this is the only fork ever placed on the right
- **NAPKIN**

Knife blades are always placed with the cutting edge toward the plate.

No more than three of any implement is ever placed on the table (with the exception of the use of an oyster fork, which makes four forks). Therefore, if more than three courses are served before dessert, the fork for the fourth course is brought in with the course; or the salad fork and knife may be omitted in the beginning and brought in when salad is served.

Dessert spoons and forks are brought in on the dessert plate just before dessert is served.

TABLECLOTHS

If you are the fortunate owner of lovely heirloom table linens, don't hide them away for fear of soiling or ruining them. Use them, for your own enjoyment and the delight of your guests. With today's cleaning processes, there are few spots that cannot be removed. Avoid trying to protect your beautiful linens by covering them with clear plastic. Not only does the plastic have an unpleasant, slippery surface, but the beauty of the cloth cannot show clearly. You might just as well buy an imitation plastic cloth and keep the good one in the drawer!

A truly formal dinner generally has a tablecloth of white damask, under which should be placed a felt pad if you wish to protect your table. If you do not have a felt pad cut to the dimensions of your table, a folded white blanket serves very well. Damask is the most conservative tablecloth, suitable in any dining room from English- and French-style to contemporary furnishings. Embroidered or lace tablecloths look nice in low-ceilinged, old-fashioned rooms. Lace and linen can go over the table without felt or other padding.

When a damask or linen cloth is used, put the middle crease on so that it is an absolutely straight line down the exact center from head to foot of the table. If it is an embroidered cloth, be sure the embroidery or monogram is right side up.

The tablecloth for a seated dinner should hang down approximately 18 inches. It should not extend to the floor, as it would on a buffet table.

NAPKINS

If you are using a damask tablecloth, then formal damask dinner napkins should match the tablecloth. Napkins are generally about 24 inches square. Whether your napkins are that size or not, they should be folded three times in each direction to make a smaller square. The two sides are then folded under, making a loosely rolled rectangle. The napkin is not flattened down completely. Care must be taken so that the monogram shows at the lower left corner of the rectangle, or if the initials are at the center of one side of the napkins, that they appear in the center third of the roll.

Smaller napkins may be folded in the same way, making only two folds to form the smaller square. Or, the smaller square may be folded in half diagonally, and the two points folded under, leaving the monogram showing in the center point.

Napkins are placed in the center of the service plate with the monogram facing the diner. They are put at the side only when a first course is put on the table before seating the guests. Putting the napkins at the side of the empty plate simply in order to display the plate is incorrect for a formal table setting. The old custom of wrapping a roll in the napkin proved impractical—a diner would often flick open a napkin and send the roll flying—and is, fortunately, considered passé today.

Napkins, if placed to the side of the plate, are never put under the forks, but rather to the left of them.

PLACE CARDS

Place cards are used to let each guest know where they are to sit at the dinner table. Some are quite formal, with the host's initials or crest monogrammed in embossed gold; others may be decorated, such as a Christmas place card with a sprig of holly pinned to it; while others are plain but employ calligraphy or a friend's handsome penmanship.

The courtesy title and surname—"Dr. Idzik," for example, or "Mr. Murphy"—are used at official dinners except when there is more than one guest with the same surname, in which case "Mr. Alan Anderson" and "Mr. Howard Anderson," for example, should be used to make the distinction. At a more informal party of friends or relatives, first names are used or, if necessary to differentiate, "Helen M." and "Helen G." The writing should be large enough to be seen easily by the guests.

Put each place card on top of and in the center of the napkin if the napkin is placed on the service plate; if it's unsteady there, place each card on the table-cloth above the service plate at the exact center of the place setting.

SILVER

It is not necessary that *all* silver match, although all forks or all spoons or all knives should be of the same pattern at one place setting. Dessert silver, which is not on the table but is brought in with the dessert plates at a formal dinner, need not match the dinner forks, and after-dinner coffee spoons are frequently entirely different. Knives with crystal or carved-bone handles may be used with any pattern.

CRYSTAL

Each place should be set with the number of glasses that will be used during the meal, with the exception of the dessert wineglass, which is put on the table after the dessert is served. Water goblets are placed closest to the center of each setting, with the wineglasses to the right in the order they will be used.

The wineglasses chosen depend, of course, on the menu, but their table-setting arrangement is according to size, so that little ones are not hidden behind large ones. The goblet for water is placed directly above the knives at the right of the plate; next to it, at a slight distance to the right, the champagne glass. In front and between these two, the claret or red wineglass, or the white wineglass; then, either in front of this or somewhat to the right again, the sherry glass. Or, instead of grouping the glasses on the table, some prefer to have them placed in a straight row slanting downward from the goblet at the upper left to the glass for sherry at the lower right.

Rarely, however, is such an impressive array of glasses seen these days except at a public dinner, which is more properly classified a banquet. At most private formal dinners two or three glasses in addition to the goblet are usual— one for sherry, one for a red wine, and one for a light white wine.

CHINA

China, too, may be mixed, but *all* the plates for each course at one table should match. For example, all the service plates must be of one pattern, although the dinner plates, while matching each other, may be entirely different. Silver or glass butter plates and glass salad or dessert plates may be used with any fine china. Each item, however, should be of the same high quality as the others. It is incorrect, for example, to use heavy pottery salad plates with fine china dinner plates, just as it is to use paper napkins with a damask tablecloth.

Although for many years butter plates were never seen on formal tables, this rule is rapidly being forgotten. Today, many people prefer their bread or roll with butter, and the idea of putting a buttered roll, or a dry one for that matter, directly onto the tablecloth is totally contrary to the aims of etiquette. Therefore, no matter how formal the dinner, the use of a butter plate is now correct. The butter plate is located above the forks at the left of the place setting.

THE FINISHING TOUCHES

Put pepper grinders and saltcellars at every place or between every two places. A set of salt-and-pepper shakers, if used instead, should be easily available to each diner; place sets two to three places apart. For a dinner of 12 there should be six (never less than four) salt and pepper shakers. Open saltcellars must be accompanied by tiny silver serving spoons, which sometimes have a gold bowl—because gold is not so easily damaged by the salt.

Most hosts prefer that their guests not smoke—or at least until coffee is served, and no ashtrays or cigarettes are placed on the table. Guests should have the good sense and courtesy to refrain until after dinner or, in the interest of everyone's health and comfort, to refrain completely unless everyone at the table is a smoker and the host has put out ashtrays.

THE INDIVIDUAL PLACES

Next comes the spacing of the individual places. The distance between places at the table must never be so short that guests have no elbow room or that the dishes cannot be served easily. When the dining-room chairs have very high backs and are placed so close as to be almost touching, it is difficult for even the most skillful server not to spill something on a guest.

Exactly how far apart do you put place settings? People who are placed one yard or more apart will find a shouted conversation equally trying. About two feet from plate center to plate center is ideal. If the chairs have narrow and low backs, people can sit much closer together. This is especially true of a small round table, the curve of which leaves a spreading wedge of space between the chairs at the back, even if the seats touch at the front corners.

LUNCHES

At an informal lunch there are few restrictions regarding table settings. Napkins may certainly be made of paper. In fact, nicer paper napkins, particularly those that are dinner size and made to resemble damask or other fabric, or which are patterned to complement your china and tablecloth, are appropriate for all but formal table settings. Candles are not needed on a lunch table, but are sometimes used as ornaments. They should not be lit in the daytime.

If the occasion is a large lunch, guests are often seated at several card tables, and place cards are used just as they are at dinner. Card tables may be covered with square tablecloths, plain or colored. A small flower arrangement makes a pretty centerpiece for each table.

For a formal luncheon, the plain white tablecloth that is correct for dinner is used, although colored damask is acceptable. Far more often, the lunch table is set with place mats made in any variety of linen, needlework, or lace. A runner, matching the mats but three or more times as long, may be used in the center of the table.

Decorations are generally the same as for dinner: Use flowers or an ornament in the center, and place two or four dishes of fruit or candy where they look best. If the table is large and appears too bare without candles, four small vases with flowers matching those in the centerpiece may be added.

The places for a large formal luncheon are set as for dinner, with a service plate, fork, knife, or spoon for each course. A luncheon napkin, which should match the tablecloth, is much smaller than a dinner napkin. Generally it is folded like a handkerchief, in a square of four thicknesses. The square is laid on the plate diagonally, with the monogrammed (or embroidered) corner pointing down toward the near edge of the table. The upper corner is then turned sharply under in a flat crease for about a quarter of its diagonal length; then the two sides are rolled loosely under, with a straight top edge and a pointed lower edge, and the monogram displayed in the center. Or, it can be folded in any simple way one prefers and placed to the left of the forks.

SEATING ARRANGEMENTS

Earlier in the century, seating arrangements were much more rigid. There were rules on where to seat the woman considered the "Lady of Most Importance" and the men deemed "First Gentleman" and "Second Gentleman." The "Lady of Next Greatest Importance" was to be taken to dinner only on the arm of the gentleman on whose right she would be sitting. It was considered bad form for two men or two women to end up sitting side by side.

It *could* get confusing. Today, of course, the rules have relaxed considerably. The general standard is to split couples up at the dinner table. This gives each person a chance to visit with someone other than who he or she came with. What may be most important, however, is not to make people unhappy—like Sam, for example, an elderly widower, who is dating a wonderful widow; at this point they can't bear to be separated. The same goes for people who may have just started dating or the occasional shy guest, whose confidence you'll want to shore up by seating him next to familiar or outgoing dining companions.

If someone is hard of hearing, consider how best to accommodate him, whether seating him with his best ear toward the conversation or beside people who speak clearly and forcefully. Lefties, too, must be given elbow room; it is thoughtful to seat a left-handed diner at a corner where his or her left arm will not bump into the person beside him when they are both eating. And while a friendly difference of opinion or even a mild argument is often stimulating, a bitter controversy is embarrassing and destructive to good conversation. It is thus safer to avoid seating people next to each other who are deeply involved in, or rabidly opinionated about, opposite sides of a controversial issue. The standard remains: Do what makes your guests most comfortable. Almost all seating problems can be worked out by common sense and an awareness of which guests will be happiest seated next to certain others. Below are some general rules on proper seating arrangements for hosts and guests at a dinner party.

- Seat honored guests at the host's and hostess's right. If the party has a female guest of honor, the host seats her on his right.
- When there is an uneven number of men and women, space them as evenly as possible. The hostess may keep her place at the end of the table unless doing so puts too many women in a row. At a formal dinner party, the woman next in importance sits at the host's left, and her husband, or the man of next importance, on the hostess's left.
- When a single woman entertains at a large dinner, she seats the female guest of honor, if there is one, at one end of the table and herself at the other end. If a man is acting as host, he is seated to the woman of honor's left. The man of

honor is seated to the hostess's right, and other guests are seated alternating men and women around the table.

- When there is more than one table, the host should sit at one table and the hostess at another. If there are more than two tables, have a good friend act as a surrogate host, seeing that wine is served and plates refilled.

P O S T N O T E S

WHICH PLATE IS WHICH?

Q. *How do I know which is the butter plate and which is the salad plate if there are two different small plates at my place setting?*

A. The butter plate is smaller and is placed above the forks while the salad plate, if served with the entrée and not as a separate course, is placed to the left of the forks.

CHAPTER 4

SETTING THE MOOD

THE DECOR: MIXING AND MATCHING

INFORMAL DECOR

The American preference for casual entertaining does not mean your decor should look thrown together. In informal entertaining, "decorating" simply means having fewer restrictions and more options in giving your table a unique appeal. Take time to come up with a decor that meshes eye-pleasing colors, textures, and materials. A table may be festooned with a gaily colored or patterned tablecloth, for example, or place mats of linen, lace, straw, or woven cotton, but all should be tied together with a universal theme—whether of color, pattern, or shape. The same theory applies to the popular trend of mixing and matching different sets of china and glassware—the practice is fine, as long as the disparate elements create a pleasing whole.

The centerpiece is another place to show your originality. Make sure your centerpiece adheres to the basic rules that formal centerpieces follow: don't let a centerpiece overwhelm a table; don't have a centerpiece that blocks the views of people sitting across from one another; don't create a centerpiece that hinders serving and dining. That, however, doesn't mean you should rely on the tried and true. It also doesn't mean you have to spend hours creating it. Beautiful ideas are usually the simplest to pull off. Thumb through magazines for some smashing centerpiece ideas—or use the following as a springboard toward making your own creative works of art.

FORMAL DECOR

The first piece to be put on the table once the cloth is in place is the centerpiece. As its name implies, it must be in the exact center. It must never be so high that diners cannot see over it, but its length and width are limited only by the size of your table. It can be composed of a wide variety of things—fresh

1. Fill straw or wicker baskets with potted African violets.
2. Combine colorful seasonal fruit, such as bananas, apples, grapes, pears, and cherries, with shiny magnolia leaves in baskets.
3. Put votive candles in small glass containers atop a mirror. Or place white candles of varying heights atop the mirror.
4. Put a long, clear glass candleholder into a clear glass vase. Fill the vase with marbles and place a candle into the candleholder. The light reflected through the marbles is truly magical.

5. At Christmas, fill clear glass bowls with Christmas ornaments and ribbon.
6. Place colorful candles atop Italian or Mexican tiles.
7. Place dried-flower or silk flower arrangements on a polished wood tabletop.
8. For a Valentine's Day table, float red or white votive candles in a large glass bowl and add red rose petals to float in the water.
9. Place a delicate medium-size vase in the center of the table, filled with fresh-cut flowers, and put a small two- to three-inch vase with one or two delicate fresh flowers at each diner's place setting.
10. At Thanksgiving, fill a large wooden bowl with gourds, squashes, and Indian corn.

flowers being the most common and surely one of the loveliest. Plastic artificial flowers are out of place, but glass, china, or silk imitation flowers or fruit are appropriate. Ornaments that need neither fruit nor flowers can be effective too, if they match the formality of the table.

Candles for the most formal dinner should be white and brand new. Only if you are skilled with a candle-tip shaper, and there is no evidence of smoke or drips, may a used candle be permissible. Candles are lit before the guests come to the table and remain lighted until they leave the dining room.

When the centerpiece is in place, a pair of candlesticks is placed at each end, about halfway between the centerpiece and the end of the table. Candlesticks or candelabra must be high and the candles as long as the proportion can stand so that the light does not shine into the eyes of those at the table.

Dishes or compotes filled with candied fruit, thin chocolate mints, or other edible trimmings may be put at the corners between the candlesticks or candelabra and the centerpiece, or wherever there are equally spaced vacancies on the table. They are left there through the entire meal and are sometimes passed around after dessert is finished. Nuts may be put on the dinner table either in large silver dishes or in small individual ones at each of the places, but they are removed with the salt-and-pepper shakers after the salad course. The colloquial description of eating "from soup to nuts" does not apply to a formal dinner. After-dessert nuts and raisins belong only on the family dinner table—especially at Thanksgiving and Christmas.

Flowers are also often seen in two or four smaller vases or epergnes, in addition to a larger arrangement in the center.

FLOWERS

There isn't any centerpiece more glorious than one that includes seasonal flowers. And now you don't have to wait for the local growing season to have fresh flowers on your table at any time of year. Most grocery-store chains have fresh flowers or plants year-round. It's also easy to order flowers from around the country through your local florist or on the Internet.

If your party is held at the height of your own backyard's blooming season, take special care of your fragile garden gems. Make sure fresh-cut flowers are given the special care they need so that you can cut them ahead of time and not find them wilting just as the party is about to start. The following are some pointers on keeping fresh-cut flowers fresh-looking and long-lasting.

- Cut flowers in the early morning or late evening and place in lukewarm water.
- Cut flower ends on the diagonal. Pluck leaves from stems that lie beneath the waterline; these can quickly rot.
- To keep freshly cut flowers fresher longer, add a couple of aspirin, a sugar cube, or a few drops of bleach.

- Keep your arrangement of flowers in a cool spot away from direct sunlight.
- Change the water in your vase every day. Revive wilted blooms by recutting stem ends and putting them in warm water and then into cool water.

CANDLES

The ambiance of a party can be greatly enhanced by soft romantic lighting. And nothing is more romantic than lit candles. It's a good idea to avoid overly aromatic candles at dinner parties because they can ruin the taste of your food. Use common sense; if it's Christmastime, candles with a mild evergreen or cinnamon aroma add to the festivities.

The number of candles you use depends on whether the room is otherwise lighted. If candles alone light a table, there should be one candle for every person. If the candles are used in addition to other lighting, two or four candles are adequate for a table of up to eight people.

Candles can be chosen by color to match a tablecloth or place mats; white or off-white candles, however, look the most elegant and are the choice for formal dinners. Festive Christmas colors are red, green, gold, and silver.

You can make ornamental candles blaze longer simply by refrigerating them for at least an hour before you use them.

Candles are used informally in candlesticks; for formal dinners, candelabra are often used, although candlesticks are fine. Make sure your candles are high enough so that the flame is above the eye level of the diners.

You should also opt for dripless candles, especially if you are using a tablecloth. Dripless candles also last longer than the nondripless types. Solid beeswax candles are smart choices; they drip inside their well and last a long time. Even with dripless candles, it's a good idea to invest in a candle snuffer or two, so that you don't risk blowing wax or sparks across the table. Some brave souls pinch the flame quickly between thumb and forefinger, and others cup their hand behind the flame and blow it out.

If candles do drip onto your nice wood tabletop, you can do something about it: Soften the wax first with a hair dryer, then combine a vinegar and water solution and sponge the drippings away. Rinse with water and dry. Don't try to scrape the wax off with a knife.

II. Parties and Events

"[When serving food] it is far better to give your guests scrambled eggs, or stew, or baked beans—any dish that is perfectly prepared—than it is to provide a pretentious menu that is indifferently well done. . . do whatever you find smoothest, simplest, and most expedient for you!"

—Emily Post, *101 Common Mistakes in Etiquette and How to Avoid Them* (1939)

CHAPTER 5

THE BIG THREE

The major forms of entertaining are generally some variation of Cocktail Party, Dinner Party, and Buffet. When choosing among "The Big Three," you'll want to consider which format best matches the purpose of your party. Then you'll want to decide how formal or informal your occasion will be, whether you'll need to hire help or not, your guest list, the type of invitations you'll need, the total budget and places to trim expenses, what foods and beverages to serve, and how to make the best use of the space you choose for your party. Once you've made all of those decisions, it's time to plot out your schedule of preparations so that your party proceeds efficiently—and you get to enjoy your own occasion.

THE COCKTAIL PARTY

In many circles, cocktails are back in fashion. Favored drinks of the '40s to the early '60s—concoctions such as the martini, the old-fashioned, and the Manhattan—are seeing a revival. Along with the new interest in cocktails is the resurgence of cocktail parties. In many parts of the country cocktail parties have become the most common form of entertaining and the answer to a busy person's quandary. Along with open houses, barbecues, and picnics, they provide a relatively simple solution to the rule that all invitations must be repaid. The cocktail party's advantages over a dinner party are many in today's society, in which relatively few households have help and the cost of hiring temporary help or a caterer is beyond the reach of many. Cocktail parties require less preparation, can be less expensive than a dinner party, have time limits, and let you entertain many more people at once in a small setting. On the other hand, no one invited to a cocktail party feels as honored as if he had been invited to dinner, and at a large party the host and hostess cannot spend as much time with any one guest as they would if they were seated at a dinner table. Cocktail parties are the perfect venue for entertaining new acquaintances and introducing them to others.

Emily Post was a teetotaler, but that didn't prevent her from attending cocktail parties and campaigning vigorously against Prohibition. She liked to call herself "a personal dry and a sopping wet." These days, a cocktail party should be stocked with nonalcoholic beverages to accommodate the nondrinkers in the crowd. Have soft drinks, juice, and seltzer on hand; you may even want to make a big pitcher of iced tea, filled with thinly sliced lemons. If, however, a invitee morally disapproves of drinking in general, he should refuse the invitation—but do so without expressing disapproval.

Cocktail parties may be as large or small, as simple or elaborate, as you wish, and the ways of inviting people are equally varied. If the number of guests is small, the invitation is almost always by telephone. For a larger party, invitations are usually written on a printed fill-in card or on an attractive store-bought card.

Unless you are having a cocktail buffet, the time is usually stated on the invitation: "Cocktails *from* 5:00 P.M. to 7:00 P.M.," rather than "Cocktails *at* 5:00 P.M." While "R.S.V.P." is often omitted, thoughtful guests let their host and/or hostess know whether or not they are planning to attend the party. If there is an R.S.V.P., the telephone number is usually written beside it, as this type of invitation may always be answered by telephone.

PLANNING THE PARTY

You may want to take the new interest in cocktails to heart when planning your party. It all depends on your guest list; if you know several people like martinis, have the ingredients ready to whip up a pitcher. If it is a Bloody Mary crowd, make up a big batch beforehand. Otherwise, stick with the basics: Scotch, bourbon, a blended whiskey, gin, vodka, rum, white wine, red wine, and beer. Stock your bar according to regional tastes, your own taste, and the taste of your guests. Also consider the season: In winter, martinis, whiskey, Scotch, and bourbon are popular drinks; white wine spritzers, cold beer, and vodka, rum, and gin mixed with tonic or fruit juices are favored in the summer. The two most important things concerning what to serve—whatever you decide on—are to have enough and to mix the drinks properly.

If the number of guests is large, have plenty of chairs available, particularly

THE WELL-STOCKED BAR

As a general rule, count on each guest having at least three drinks. A o[...] will provide 21 1½-ounce drinks or serve approximately seven people. M[...] stores will let you return unopened bottles, so always buy a bit more than you need. Don't forget the nonalcoholic drinks, including tomato and fruit juices, a choice of sodas, and sparkling mineral waters. It's important to base your selections on what you know about your guests' preferences. Many people these days prefer wine to liquor, for example.

At a large party have plenty of extra glasses on hand. Guests continually put down their glasses and forget where they put them, or leave their empty ones behind when they go to the bar for another drink. Plastic glasses are perfectly fine—and perfectly practical—to use for a big informal party. And don't forget perhaps the most important ingredient: ice, and plenty of it!

The well-stocked bar should include:

- MIXERS AND FIXINGS lemons, limes, olives, tonic, seltzer or club soda, sweet and dry vermouth, bitters, orange juice, tomato juice, grapefruit juice
- PAPER/PLASTIC GOODS napkins, glasses, toothpicks, coasters
- ESSENTIAL ACCOUTREMENTS jigger, corkscrew, swizzle sticks, bottle opener, bar towel, ice bucket, cocktail spoon or stirrer, paring knife, small cutting board, cocktail picks

For every 10 guests have:

- Three fifths each of vodka, scotch, and bourbon—or the liquors favored by your guests
- Five bottles of wine
- Five six-packs of beer
- Five six-packs of soda

for those who have difficulty standing for long periods of time. You don't have to have chairs for everyone—otherwise you'd have to line them up along the walls or place them in rows. Guests expect to stand for periods of time at a large cocktail party, and not being rooted in a seat enables them to move from group to group—which is one of the social purposes of a cocktail party. When there are few (six to 10) guests, the conversation tends to be general among the group, and most people gravitate to couches and chairs. In this case, ensure that there are enough chairs available for everyone.

COCKTAIL PARTY FOOD

At a cocktail party, think finger food. You may serve literally any sort of hors d'oeuvre or appetizer that you think tastes good and looks tempting, as long as it can be eaten with little fuss. One-bite foods, mini appetizers, and morsels that can be picked up with a toothpick are all perfect cocktail party foods. Small puff pastries, stuffed mushrooms, and dips and crudités are good choices. At some cocktail parties small plates and forks are placed on the hors d'oeuvres table so that guests can fill these plates with food. Often this creates a difficult, if not impossible, situation for the guest, who has to hold a drink in one hand, the plate in the other, and somehow manage to eat the hors d'oeuvres and even shake hands at the same time. Have plenty of paper napkins lying around, nonetheless.

When selecting your appetizers, keep your guests' considerations in mind. Make sure to have a number of vegetable choices for the vegetarians in the group. Ethnic cuisines have become popular, as have lighter, more health-conscious foods. More choices are available as well; drag your crudités dish into the twenty-first century with fresh baby vegetables and exotic fruits. That doesn't mean you have to turn your back on the still-popular standards like chicken wings and cheese balls; it just means you should offer a range of choices for all palates and preferences.

A COCKTAIL PARTY WITHOUT HELP

Generally, the host and hostess of a cocktail party serve as bartender and server, dividing the duties between them. Hors d'oeuvres can be passed around or offered on a table for the guests to help themselves.

If you are the designated bartender for the evening, you should ask each guest as he arrives what he would like to drink. If the choice is limited you may say, "Will you have a martini or Scotch?" rather than "What would you like?" This saves both of you from the embarrassment of having the guest request a drink that you don't have. You may also invite your guests to refill their own glasses if they want another drink. Just be sure to have a jigger, for measuring quantities, readily available. A self-serve bar will help free up your time to visit and perform your other duties.

If your party has only a few guests, you may hang their coats in a hall closet. If there are more wraps than a closet can conveniently hold, ask your guests to put them on a bed in a bedroom.

Either the host or the hostess should always stay within sight of the door to greet arriving guests—but should at the same time try to avoid being out of the room where the party is held. Try not to greet new guests at the door with drinks in your hands.

10 EASY COCKTAIL PARTY HORS D'OEUVRES

You don't have to spend hours in the kitchen in order to have delicious, enticing food at your cocktail party. All of the following hors d'oeuvres can be prepared ahead of time or at the last minute.

- Mozzarella balls marinated in basil and olive oil
- Mini ham biscuits with honey mustard
- Sun-dried tomato and sour cream dip with raw vegetables
- Deviled eggs with a dollop of salmon roe (inexpensive) or caviar (expensive)
- Smoked salmon and cream cheese on mini toast pieces or thin slices of pumpernickel
- Spicy cheese sticks
- A dip of artichokes, mayonnaise, and Parmesan cheese served with crackers
- Homemade salsa and chips
- Potato chips, pretzels, and trail mix

BARTENDERS AND SERVERS

If you are planning a cocktail party for more than 18 or 20 people, it is wise to consider hiring a bartender for the evening. One bartender can serve between 20 and 30 people quite nicely. If the party is larger, you may want to hire two bartenders and locate each at separate bar areas—the crush around one can become unmanageable. If you have two bars, you can designate one as strictly a cocktail bar and the other for wine, beer, and nonalcoholic drinks only.

At a large cocktail party, guests generally go to the bar themselves and request the kind of drink they wish. Make sure your bar is stocked with plenty of ice, cocktail glasses, wineglasses, and beer mugs. If you have two people to serve drinks, but only one bar, have one person making the mixed drinks and the other pouring wine. Or have one person be on cleanup duty, discarding any empty glasses or dishes.

Be sure to instruct the bartender in advance exactly how you like your drinks mixed and insist that he use a measure, or jigger. A jigger measures out a precise 1.5 ounces of liquor, the standard serving for cocktails and highballs. If you let your bartender measure by eye, you may find that your liquor supply is about to run out long before the cocktail hour is over. Or you may have some unexpectedly boisterous guests on your hands!

Make sure your bartender wraps a napkin around each glass, whether a fresh drink or a refill. Napkins prevent drips and make holding a wet, icy glass more comfortable. Have plenty of coasters in sight to prevent damage to table-tops.

Many people enlist the help of friends to tend bar; if you do, you can present each with a small gift at the end of the evening as a thank you for their efforts.

COCKTAIL BUFFETS

A cross between a cocktail party and a buffet dinner party, the cocktail buffet is the choice of many for entertaining all but the smallest and most informal groups. Because a cocktail buffet generally has plenty of food, guests won't need to make plans for dinner and can linger longer at the party. Thus, a cocktail buffet invitation frequently states only the hour of arrival. In many sections of the country this is likely to be a little later than a simple cocktail party, often at 6:30 P.M. or 7:00 P.M. But do make it clear on the invitation that the gathering is a cocktail buffet.

The menu may vary from simple to elaborate, but even the simplest provides more than just hors d'oeuvres. If you don't want to deal with china and silver, choose food that can be eaten in small bites, such as meatballs or frank-furters, or speared with a toothpick, such as shrimp. Chicken wings, for instance, require receptacles for discards but no utensils. Tacos are hearty and the shells can be bought frozen. Slices of meat can be placed on a piece of bread and eaten like a sandwich, and raw vegetables can be picked up and dipped in a sauce.

A pretty buffet table may be covered with a tablecloth and, if there is room, a centerpiece of flowers or fruit. For a more elaborate buffet you might include one or more hot casseroles that can be kept warm on an electric hot plate or served in a chafing dish over a flame. If the main table is too crowded, put the hot dishes on a sideboard or a side table. The main difference between this type of cocktail buffet and a buffet dinner is that only one real course is served, although cookies or cake may be offered with coffee.

THE DINNER PARTY

Emily Post's phenomenal success with the publishing of *Etiquette* in 1922 quickly turned this mother of two sons into an American icon. "Emily Post has ceased to be a person and has become a noun, a synonym for etiquette and manners," wrote columnist Jeanne Perkins in 1946. Meeting the great Emily Post for the first time was an intimidating prospect for many. Once, a newspaper reporter, petrified at the thought of meeting with the country's number-one social arbiter over dinner, stepped into a bar beforehand for some liquid courage. When he arrived at Mrs. Post's apartment, she graciously offered him a drink. Being a gracious guest, he couldn't refuse. When the reporter, now thoroughly inebriated, finally sat down to eat, he sent his lamb chop flying across the table.

"You wrote the book," he said pleadingly. "What do I do?"

"If I were you," Mrs. Post replied unblinkingly, "I would pick it up and start all over again."

The lesson? Make your guests feel comfortable, never intimidated. Poise and graciousness in the face of potential disaster can smooth out any awkward patches.

THE SUCCESSFUL DINNER PARTY

Whether your dinner party is held in a restaurant, a club, or your own home, and whether there are 100 guests or eight, the requisites for a successful occasion are the same. They are:

- GUESTS who are congenial.
- A MENU that is well planned and suited to your guests' tastes.
- AN ATTRACTIVE TABLE with everything in perfect condition: linen pressed, silver polished, and glassware sparkling.

- **FOOD** that is well prepared.
- **A GRACIOUS AND CORDIAL HOSTESS AND HOST,** who are welcoming and at the same time enjoy their guests

Most well-planned dinner parties go off without a hitch. Fiascoes, however, do happen to everyone sooner or later. No matter what occurs, it's all about making a gracious recovery—whether for your guests or for yourself—and having a sense of humor.

We've all experienced the ice-cold ovens and the collapsing soufflés—if dinner falls flat, just order a couple of pizzas and put your feet up; the whole evening will be next year's dinner-party anecdote.

The best hosts make it look so easy. Here is some gold-plated advice on preparing food for a smashing dinner party:

1. Plan ahead.
2. Serve something you've served before.
3. Have a fallback—if the dessert soufflé falls, have ice cream and fudge sauce in the kitchen as a backup.

THE INFORMAL DINNER PARTY

The need to break bread among friends is built into our genes. But with today's 70-hour workweek, two-career and single-parent households, and a society that is constantly on the move, it has become harder and harder to fit social occasions into our crowded schedules. Giving a fancy dinner party, in the traditional sense, can be a tremendous amount of work. Maybe that's why most dinner parties today are more informal.

Modern conveniences and easy access to quality foods make it easier to entertain friends and loved ones around the dinner table, in the relaxed, informal style so favored today by on-the-go Americans. "Informal" can mean a range of things, from a sit-down candlelit dinner of several courses to a served-from-the-stove one-pot-meal affair.

Planning the Menu

When choosing your dinner-party menu, always strive to plan a well-balanced meal. Don't serve heavy or spicy dishes back to back. Balance an especially rich dish with a simple one. Coquilles St. Jacques (scallops in a thick cream sauce), for example, might be followed by simply grilled medallions of lamb; a pasta carbonara followed by lemony broiled fish. Combine flavors intelligently. Don't serve an assortment of spicy food, or your guests' palates will never recover. Don't serve successive sweet dishes, such as duck basted with currant jelly, a fruit salad, and a raspberry trifle for dessert. Each dish may be delicious all by itself but is unappetizing in the monotony of its combination.

A second consideration is the appearance of the food you serve. Avoid a dinner of white sauces from beginning to end: Don't follow a creamed soup, for example, with breast of chicken and mashed potatoes. Color is as important in devising your menu as it is in planning your decor. What, indeed, is prettier than a plate where a summer-ripe tomato rests on a deep green bed of spinach, surrounded by slices of yellow squash and topped with a shrimp salad flecked with bits of bright green chives?

Consider as well the season. Light foods, such as main-course salads and cold soups, are perfect warm-weather fare. Heavy foods, such as stews and roasts, warm the soul in winter. Make use of the season in another way by creating a menu using fresh seasonal foods. In autumn, take advantage of butternut and acorn squash; in winter, Brussels sprouts are at their peak; in spring, soft-shell crabs are a favored delicacy and beautiful fresh asparagus floods the market. Summer brings a bounty of fresh vegetables; conceivably an entire meal could be based around fresh summer foods.

Finally, in planning your menu, consider the limitations of your kitchen. If you have only one oven and plan to cook a roast, don't also plan dishes that must be cooked in the oven at the same time but under different temperatures and different cooking times. So, instead of planning a baked vegetable casserole or biscuits, for example, prepare a salad, sauté squash, steam vegetables, or mash potatoes on the stove. If your space is limited, prepare what you can ahead of time and plan your cooking times carefully so that no dish is delayed by a shortage of mixing, cooking, or carving space.

While assessing your kitchen, think about pots and pans. If you're serving a large group, you may need bigger-size pots than your own. You can find over-size stainless-steel pots at good prices at restaurant-supply stores, or you can rent them.

Before-Dinner Drinks

When predinner drinks or cocktails are served, dinner should be planned for at least an hour later than the time noted on the invitation; 20 minutes later if drinks are not served, which allows late arrivals a moment of relaxation.

Two or three varieties of cocktails should be offered, with the bartender or host indicating what they are. Wine should be offered too, for those who prefer it to hard liquor. Don't forget to provide soda, juices, and sparkling water for the nondrinkers in the crowd. Generally, your guests should have time for one or two cocktails.

Many dinner parties with a cocktail hour offer light snacks or hors d'oeuvres with the drinks. They may be hot or cold and either served, offered at the bar, or scattered around on the room's various tables. Make sure the flavors are compatible with the food you plan to serve at dinner.

The Late Guest

Don't let a late guest disrupt your dinner-party schedule. Fifteen minutes is the established length of time that a hostess need delay her dinner for a late guest. To wait more than 20 minutes, at the outside, would be showing rudeness to many for the sake of one. When the late guest finally enters the dining room, he must apologize to the hostess right away for being late. The latecomer is served whatever course is being eaten at the time he arrives. If that happens to be dessert, however, the hostess makes sure the main course is served to him first.

Dinner Is Served

When dinner is ready to be served, the candles are lit and water glasses are filled. Try to have the first course, if it is not a hot dish, already served at each diner's place. When it is time, simply announce, "Dinner is ready; shall we go in?" if the group is small. If the group is large, you may ask two or three good friends to help you move the other guests toward the dining room. If you are having difficulty getting people to respond, suggest that guests bring their cocktails to the table. They no longer have an excuse to delay. Then you lead the way in to dinner.

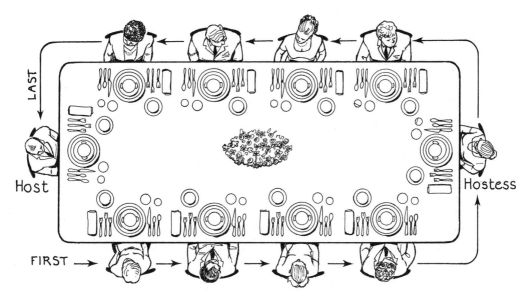

The female guest of honor seated on the host's right is always served each dish first. If there is serving help, servers move around the table counterclockwise from her, serving the host last. The hostess is never served first.

When food is served directly from the kitchen, service is also counterclockwise from the female to the host's right, with the host served last. Plates are served from the guests' left side and removed, if possible, from the right. (An easy way to remember this is "R.R."—remove right.)

Each dish is supplied with whatever silver is needed for serving it. A serving spoon and a large fork are put on most dishes, or the spoon alone is used if the dish is not hard to serve. With the spoon underneath, the fork is held with the prongs turned down to hold and balance the portion when both utensils are used.

At a more casual dinner party, you may simply let guests serve themselves or at least pass the potato and vegetable dishes around the table instead. If the salad has not been served on individual salad plates, then it can be served from a large salad bowl passed from guest to guest, with each guest in turn holding it for the person on his right.

Since any of these procedures can take considerable time—time in which the food can grow cold—it is important that the host or hostess insist that guests start eating after three or four people have been served. If the host and hostess forget to do so, a guest is perfectly correct in beginning to eat.

The Big Three

Except at formal dinners, bread and other condiments are usually passed around the table by the guests themselves. Dishes are passed counterclockwise to the right and should be passed in the same direction, simply to keep the process orderly. A guest helps himself to the bread basket with his fingers and lays the roll or bread on his butter plate. If there is a choice of two or three sauces or other condiments, placing them together in a divided dish, or on a small, easily managed tray, ensures that they are passed together and all guests are aware of the choices.

Dessert may be served already placed on individual dessert plates, or the hostess may serve it at the table.

When the table is cleared by the hostess alone or with a close friend assisting, dishes are removed two at a time, never stacked. Salt-and-pepper containers and condiment dishes are cleared also. To accelerate the clearing process, it is quite correct to bring back dessert plates, or whatever is needed for the next course, when you return from the kitchen. Or have a friend serve the dessert while you finish clearing.

Second Helpings

If you have a sideboard or serving table, use it as a halfway station between the dinner table and the kitchen. On it you can have plates for the next course and extra flatware. Serving dishes, after being passed, can be left on the serving table on a warming tray or taken to the kitchen and kept warm on the stove. When you see that guests are ready for another portion, get up, get the serving bowl and pass it around.

Clearing the Table

Salad plates as well as the plates used for the entrée are removed before dessert is served. Any salt-and-pepper shakers, unused flat silver, and dishes of nuts are taken off (on a serving tray, if you like).

It is safest to remove dishes two at a time. Never stack or scrape the dishes at the table. As mentioned above, each time something is taken to the kitchen, you may bring back dessert plates, salad and salad plates, or whatever is needed. If you wish, you may put a dessert plate at each place you have cleared as you return to take the next plate, or you may serve the dessert at the table.

To guests who offer to help you clear, just say, "No, thank you, really it is easier to do it myself"—or you may find that everyone is suddenly on his or her feet and in the kitchen. It's better to designate a serving and cleaning buddy in advance to help—a son or daughter, a close friend—but your other guests should be just that, guests, and remain at the table.

After-Dinner Coffee

After-dinner coffee may be served either at the dining table or in another room to which the diners have moved. Customarily, the hostess pours the coffee (and sometimes tea) right at the dining-room table or from a tray that has been carried to the living room or den. Serving coffee is more complicated today than it was in Emily Post's day, when real coffee was served with real cream and real sugar—no choices, no questions. As people have become more conscious about their health, the choices and questions have multiplied. Now after-meal choices include regular coffee; brewed or instant decaffeinated coffee; regular, flavored, or herbal teas; cream, whole milk, or skim milk; sugar or sugar substitutes; lemon for tea; even cappuccino and espresso, caffeinated or not. In deciding what to offer, today's hostess generally considers the preferences of her guests. When giving a small dinner for friends whom she knows drink only decaffeinated coffee, the choice is simple. When entertaining a larger group, the hostess should offer a variety of options, perhaps a pot of brewed coffee, a pot of decaffeinated coffee, and a pot of hot water with a selection of teas.

After-Dinner Drinks

Some hosts like to serve after-dinner drinks with coffee. If coffee is served at the table, bottles of after-dinner drinks may also be placed on the table, often on a tray holding a variety of glasses. Each guest is then asked which he or she would prefer. If coffee is served in the living room, the tray containing the bottles and glasses is placed on the coffee table, and a choice is offered to each guest.

When dinner is over you don't need to clear the dessert dishes unless your dining table is at one end of the living room. In that case, quickly remove the dessert dishes so you won't subject your guests to the unappetizing sight of dirty dishes for the rest of the evening. Do not, however, abandon your guests and start washing dishes immediately after dinner is over—no matter how compulsively neat you are—nor should you permit your guests to insist on washing them. Every meal produces dishes to be washed; since you have invited friends to your home to enjoy a pleasant visit—not to have them do the same chores they must do every day at home—just thank them for the offer but politely insist that you'll deal with the dishes later.

THE FORMAL DINNER PARTY

Today, in these most informal times, almost any dinner where guests are seated at a dining-room table and served by someone other than themselves is considered a formal dinner. Of course there are still degrees of formality, dependent upon the dress, table setting, food served, and type of service. In 1922 Emily Post considered it impossible to give a formal dinner without the help of servants. Yet today the hostess who single-handedly cooks a perfectly prepared meal and serves it at a beautifully set table is considered to have given a formal dinner.

There are official formal dinners, which must follow certain rules and are given only by diplomats or people in very high public positions. In those cases rules of protocol and precedence are strictly followed. There are protocol offices and written guidelines to help those who are unacquainted with the requirements. Newcomers to the world of diplomacy can get the information they need through the Office of Protocol in Washington, D.C., or from *The Green Book*, published each year in the Washington area, with all the current social information a hostess needs to know—names, titles, rules of precedence. Embassies and consulates also have staff members who can provide protocol information.

For most of us, a formal dinner does not require adherence to official protocol; it provides a framework around which to develop your own brand of entertaining. By taking the suggestions that appeal to you, by eliminating the details that would be unnatural or difficult for you, and by combining the elements that are suitable to your home and your friends, you can use the information that follows just as it should be used—as a guide. Remember always: It is far less important to have matching silver or fine goblets than it is to be a warm, relaxed, and gracious party giver. Self-confidence helps you to be all these things, and a knowledge that you are doing things correctly—to the very best of your ability—will give you the assurance to entertain easily and well.

Guests: Greeting and Seating

At large formal dinners, guests are often greeted at the door by a housekeeper or temporary help, who then takes their coats. The hostess stands in the living room, near the door. As guests enter, she greets them with a smile and a handshake and welcomes them. The host, who is circulating and talking to other guests, excuses himself and comes to greet each newcomer as soon as he can. Predinner drinks are then served to the guests. After the cocktail hour, all guests are invited to proceed to the dining room.

The hostess is always the last to go into the dining room when place cards are used. (Place cards are always used at very formal dinners, but they are also useful at any dinner so large that the hostess cannot easily indicate where everyone is to sit.) If there are no place cards, the hostess indicates where guests are to sit. Women sit down as soon as they find their places, even though the hostess remains standing until everyone is at his chair. Men hold the chairs for the women on their right. The men do not sit down until the hostess is seated. The male guest of honor, even though he has escorted the hostess in, seats the woman on his right, and the man on the hostess's left seats her.

There are two key considerations in deciding where guests are to be seated. First, seat honored guests at the host's and hostess's right. For example, if the party has a female guest of honor, the host seats her on his right; the male guest of honor is seated at the hostess's right. Second, seat your guests according to whatever arrangement you think they will enjoy the most. There are many choices for determining who sits where. Many hosts like to alternate men and women, and separate husbands and wives. It's up to you, as host, to decide on the most advantageous way to arrange your guests so that the mix will contribute to a pleasant experience.

Formal Service

At a very formal dinner served by a staff, one server generally stands behind the hostess's chair, except when pouring wine. At a smaller dinner one server will handle everything himself; or, if he has a server to help him, he passes the principal dishes and the server follows with the accompanying dishes.

In any case, whether there are two diners or 300, plates are changed and courses presented in precisely the same manner. No serving dishes or platters are ever put on the table except ornamental compotes of fruit or candy. The meat is carved in the kitchen or pantry; vegetables, bread, and condiments are passed and returned to a side table or the kitchen.

From the time the table is set until it is cleared for dessert, a service plate should remain at every place. For the first course, the plate on which oysters or clams are served is put on top of the service plate (also called a charger), as is a plate holding fruit or cold seafood in a stemmed glass if they, instead, are served as the first course. At the end of the course the used plate is removed, leaving the service plate. The soup plate is also put on top of this same plate. But when the soup plate is removed, the plate underneath is removed with it, and the hot plate for the main course is immediately exchanged for the two taken away.

The only plates that are properly brought into the dining room one-in-each-hand are for soup and dessert. The soup plates are put down on the service plates, which have not been removed, and the dessert plates are put down on the tablecloth. The plates of every other course have to be exchanged, and therefore each individual service requires two hands at a time. Soup plates carried two at a time can be dangerous—a mishap can occur while putting down one plate. If only one plate of soup is brought in at a time, accidents should not happen. Also, the spoon and fork on the dessert plate can easily fall off unless it is held level. Two plates at a time are therefore not a question of etiquette, but one of the server's skill.

THE SERVICE PLATE AND HOW TO USE IT

When a service plate is used at a formal dinner, from the time the table is set until it is cleared for dessert, a plate should remain on the table at every place. The meal starts with a service plate (also referred to as a charger), a large plate usually 12 inches in diameter. The service plate at each place is a base for the first course, which is served on a separate plate that is put on top of the service plate. When the first course is cleared, the service plate remains until the hot plate with the entrée is served, at which time the two plates (the service plate and the entrée plate) are exchanged.

Clearing the Table

Although all dishes are presented at the left of the person being served, it is better that plates be removed from the right. If more convenient, however, it is permissible to remove them from the left. Glasses are refilled as necessary. Additional knives are placed at the right, while forks are put on as needed at the left. Crumbs are brushed off each place with a tightly folded napkin onto a small tray or a silent butler held under the table edge.

At one time proper service required the removal of each plate the instant the fork was laid down on it, so that by the time the last diner was finished, the entire table was set with clean plates and was ready for the next course. But the protests of the slow eaters were loud and clear, and a considerate hostess now does not have any plates removed until the slowest eaters have finished.

Formal Dinner Courses

Six courses are the maximum for even the most elaborate formal dinner. They are:

1. **SOUP, FRESH FRUIT CUP, SLICED MELON, OR SHELLFISH** (such as clams, oysters, or shrimp)
2. **FISH COURSE** unless shellfish is served first
3. **THE ENTRÉE** or main course (usually roast meat or fowl and vegetables)
4. **SALAD** The salad is served between the entrée and the dessert. This is correct, in spite of the custom in almost all American restaurants of serving salad as a first course. Unless you know that a group of friends prefer it first, salad should be served toward the end of the meal or may be served with the entrée, on a separate salad plate.
5. **DESSERT** There are two methods of serving dessert. One is to put the dessert fork and spoon on the dessert plate. If the dessert is served in a glass bowl, the bowl is placed on the plate before it is served. If finger bowls are used, they are brought on another plate after dessert has been served. Another formal way to serve dessert is to bring the finger bowl, as well as the fork and spoon, on a small doily on the dessert plate. The diner puts the finger bowl, with the doily, to the left above his plate and places the fork and spoon each to its proper side. After dessert, the diner dips his fingers, one hand at a time, into the water and then dries his fingers on his napkin.

   When fresh fruit is to be served it is passed after the dessert, and decorative sweets, such as mints, are passed last.
6. **COFFEE** can be served with after-dinner drinks.

THE BUFFET

Buffets are grand fun for everyone. Hosting a buffet is, in today's parlance, entertaining interactively. There are three great advantages to a buffet dinner that appeal to many. First, you can accommodate more guests than your dining-room table will seat. That doesn't mean you should go wild, however. It is important to restrict the number so that there will be places for everyone to sit down, and enough elbow room for guests to move about freely.

Second, lack of service is no handicap. Because a buffet is truly a do-it-yourself party, even the hostess without help may spend almost the entire evening with her guests. It gives her the luxury of preparing meals well in advance: the cooked ham, the potato salad, the crispy cheese wafers.

And third, a buffet is blessed with the informality that many of us prefer today. There is something about sitting in one place before dinner, going into the dining room and foraging for yourself, then coming back to the same place or finding a new place, as you prefer, that makes buffet parties so popular. Also, you are free to choose your dinner companions yourself, something you cannot do at a seated dinner.

Start

DECORATING THE BUFFET TABLE

Set your buffet table as formally or informally as you wish. A white damask cloth, silver candelabra, and white roses will make your buffet appear quite formal. But you can just as well go to the other extreme. It's fun and appetizing to see pottery dishes on a checked tablecloth with a bowl of fruit in the center of the table. What makes your table attractive is not only the elegance of the utensils and decorations you use, but the combination of dishes, linen, and silver, and the way in which they are arranged.

Color plays an enormous part in the beauty of a buffet table. If you have a copper bowl or kettle, use it as a centerpiece filled with red and yellow fruit or a combination of vegetables—squash, tomatoes, gourds, and pumpkins—for a festive Halloween or Thanksgiving table. Keep the autumn tints in mind when you choose accompanying mats and tablecloth; use yellow, orange, or russet mats, for example, and wooden bowls on a bare table. A Christmas buffet shines with gold-flecked garlands around each dish. Vases filled with white and red chrysanthemums set the tone for an appealing Valentine's Day table.

SETTING THE BUFFET TABLE

When space is precious, use only necessary and useful objects. Unless there is ample space, articles that are solely ornamental are a minor consideration. If your choice for a focal point is between a flower arrangement and a bowl of fruit, a centerpiece of fruit to be served for dessert is the smarter choice. Of course, you can always create innovative containers out of edible foods: a pumpkin half filled with shrimp salad, for example.

In the same way, if the table is crowded and candles are not needed to see by, don't use them. If candles are needed to illuminate the food, try candelabra instead of individual candlesticks—first, they provide superior light, and second, they are less likely to be knocked over by a guest reaching for a serving bowl or platter.

If the party is large and the room is big enough, it is better to leave the table in the center of the room so that two lines of guests may serve themselves on both sides of the table at once. Divide each dish into two platters, and mirror them on either side of the table. First divide the main course into two parts, and place one platter or casserole at each end of the table. Plates are set in two stacks beside each platter, and napkins and silver neatly arranged next to each

The Big Three

set of plates. Place twin dishes of vegetables, salads, bread and butter, and sauces and condiments on both sides of the table so that guests need only pass down one side—which greatly speeds the service and keeps guests from turning back and bumping into one another. If the table is set against the wall, place your plates and main dish at the end that makes for the best flow of traffic.

THE BUFFET MENU

The foods you choose for your buffet should be well prepared, easy to manage with fork alone if your guests are not seated at tables, and ones that don't need to be eaten immediately out of the frying pan or grill (like a charbroiled steak). Beyond that, simply use common sense in selecting dishes for a buffet. French fries can get soggy, for example, while stuffed potatoes work fine. Avoid dishes that are soupy, that wilt or collapse, or need to be buttered. Consider, too, the type of buffet you're having: you'll want heavier food, and more of it, at a dinner buffet; a lighter menu at lunch; finger foods at a cocktail party. Guests should keep in mind, however, that it is easy to overload a plate when there is a variety of tempting dishes. If you are a guest at a buffet, don't let your eyes overrule your stomach; help yourself to small portions, and if you're still hungry, you can get seconds later.

If you are serving hot food, the most valuable piece of equipment you can have is one that keeps things hot. An electric hot plate or tray is recommended, because it can be used to heat your plates and keep your meal warm in the kitchen for an almost indefinite period of time. As long as a finished casserole is covered (to keep it from drying out), it can be placed on a hot plate an hour or more before dinner and be as delectable when it is served as it was the moment it was taken from the oven. Have an electric warming tray on the buffet table to keep food warm for second helpings. With electric appliances, you don't have to spend time replacing fuel for flame-heated chafing dishes. Make sure, however, that cords are not a trip hazard for guests.

You can get around the hot-plate dilemma by offering food that can be eaten at room temperature or chilled. A dinner of cold sliced steak with horseradish sauce, poached salmon with dill sauce, a rice salad, and marinated vegetables make a hot-plate buffet a moot point.

BUFFET BEVERAGES

Place beverages and glasses on a separate sideboard or nearby table, if possible. If you are having a seated buffet, place water glasses on the tables and fill them before the guests sit down. Wineglasses should also be at the guests' places, but should never be filled in advance. The host (or a server) passes the wine when everyone is seated, or an opened bottle of wine can be placed on each table, to be poured by the person nearest to it.

If coffee is on the sideboard, guests may serve themselves at any time. Or the host or hostess can take a tray set with cups, a coffeepot, cream, and sugar into the living room to serve after dinner.

Coasters should be provided so that glasses are not put directly on table-tops. When there are no individual stands or tables and guests must put their glasses beside them on the floor, it is wise to use iced-tea glasses or highball glasses because they are steadier than goblets.

SERVING THE MEAL

When the guests have all arrived and the time allotted for cocktails (if served) is over, the hostess announces that dinner is ready. Guests, who are always served before the host and hostess, should form a line around the dining table, helping themselves to the selections. It is always a nice gesture to offer to fill the plate for the elders or those who may be incapacitated.

Once guests have served themselves, they simply take their plates and sit wherever the hosts have designated guests to sit. Ideally, there should be enough room for every guest to be able to sit down, hold a plate, or set a glass down on the nearest table. Avoid accidents and make your guests more comfortable by placing a small table (the folding kind that fit in a rack are ideal and easy to store) near each chair, or at least by any chair that is not within easy reach of a coffee or side table.

At some buffets, guests may be seated at the dining table and/or at small tables set up for the occasion. Set the places exactly as you would for any seated dinner. A big plus: Since the guests need not carry silver, napkins, or glasses with them, a great deal of space is saved on the buffet table. Guests serve themselves as at all buffets, going for second helpings, and removing their empty plates unless there is a server to do so. If small tables have been placed around the room, they are removed after the meal to provide space for conversational

The Big Three

groups or any planned activities. This arrangement is, of course, dependent on your having enough space so that tables are neither crowded nor in the way.

The only serving detail of importance in a buffet meal is the clearing away of used dishes. The host or hostess may enlist the help of a friend or two to assist in taking used dishes to a convenient table or sideboard. From there the dishes can be carried to the kitchen as unobtrusively as possible. At a very informal buffet where family and close friends are the guests, nothing is wrong with guests carrying their empty plates to the kitchen themselves rather than waiting for them to be collected.

P O S T   N O T E S

MIX IT YOURSELF

Q. *How can I discourage my guests from mixing their own drinks?*

A. It is difficult to do without being insulting. You can control the situation somewhat, however, by going to the bar with them and asking them to get out the ice or the mix while you pour the liquor yourself. You can also avoid having more than one bottle of liquor in evidence if guests seem to be heavy drinkers, or you can make it obvious that you use a jigger to pour drinks by handing the jigger to your guests before they pour for themselves.

CHAPTER 6

HOLIDAY GATHERINGS

Holidays are the most festive and spiritual times of the year, where time-honored rituals are played out and enjoyed by successive generations. Holidays are also the times of the year when families make every effort to gather together, no matter how far apart they live or how seldom they see one another. This is borne out in most family photographs, where the lights of a Christmas tree twinkle merrily in the background or where little ones preen in Easter finery. However we celebrate, the holidays are special occasions that resonate with meaning and joy.

CHRISTMAS OPEN HOUSE

An open house is literally what the name implies. The door is open to all those invited at any time between the hours stated on the invitation. Most open houses these days are held to celebrate a holiday. A particularly popular holiday for an open house is Christmas.

Personal invitations are generally sent out on informal or commercial cards bought for the occasion. When invitations are issued in church or club announcements, the host is saved from having to invite the entire membership individually.

Most holiday open houses don't request an R.S.V.P.—if anything, invitations may include a "Regrets only." Refreshments range from the simple—dips, sandwiches, bowls of nuts, and punch—to elaborate buffets containing country hams, fresh biscuits, cheese puffs, and bowls of shrimp. Because most holiday cocktail parties and open houses offer staggered times so guests can come and go, guests at open houses generally stay no more than an hour. It's perfectly correct to attend more than one holiday party in the same evening—unless one of the parties is a dinner party or a small gathering, with a set time to arrive or a limited number of guests.

A holiday open house is likely to be decorated with all the trimmings of the season; the food also follows a holiday theme. Eggnog, grog, or wassail are traditional drinks at a Christmas open house, and a bowl of eggnog may be surrounded by sprigs of seasonal greenery. A platter of Christmas cookies is a holiday party staple. Christmas music, whether live or taped, may be part of the festivities.

Often the holiday open house is a tree-trimming. If you're invited to a Christmas tree trimming, you should bring the hosts a new ornament to hang on the tree. Some hosts throw caroling parties, where guests begin and end at the host's home for refreshments. In between, the party strolls the neighborhood singing Christmas carols. The host should provide flashlights or short candles for participants to hold; if candles are used, plastic coffee lids make great drip trays for each candle. A fire in the fireplace and hot buttered rum combine to make a warm greeting for the night's carolers.

NEW YEAR'S DAY BEAN PARTY

New Year's Eve is one big party. Even if you choose to celebrate at home alone with your family, the ticking of the clock at midnight marks a festive time. For many people, then, the wisdom of a sedate and relaxed New Year's Day gathering—after the excitement of the previous evening—becomes apparent.

The custom of serving good-luck beans on New Year's Day has its roots in rituals performed by early African Americans, who left beans in pots on roadsides as gifts to the gods for good luck. Today, in the southern United States, hopping John (usually field peas and rice) or black-eyed peas simmered with vegetables and ham hocks is a New Year's Day good-luck ritual.

Greet the New Year with close friends and family by having your own Bean Party. People are invited to come dressed casually. You can include brunch food, orange and grapefruit juices, beer, wine, and champagne. Use paper goods to serve food. Have the New Year's Day football bowl games on the television. And have a big pot of good-luck beans simmering on the stove, and let guests serve themselves.

FOURTH OF JULY

On this festive summer evening, backyards across America light up with all the traditional talismans of the Fourth of July: hamburgers on the grill; red, white, and blue flags; and sparklers and fireworks. Much like the Thanksgiving turkey and Christmas evergreens, Fourth of July rituals are comforting constants in our lives.

This is a perfect holiday for a neighborhood or community to share hosting duties. Have someone on your block offer the use of his backyard, or close off a street (get the necessary permits from the local government first) and have a Fourth of July street party. Borrow or rent long tables from local churches or schools, cover with red-and-white checkered plastic tablecloths, string up Japanese lanterns, and get out the grill for a meal of hamburgers and hot dogs. Offer watermelons, bowls of strawberries and blueberries, and grilled corn on the cob. Someone might put blueberries and strawberries in water-filled ice-cube trays and use the frozen cubes in drinks. Set aside a kids' area for games and activities, and a separated area for the sparklers and for adults to set off small fireworks. A word about safety: Before celebrating with fireworks, check with local laws and ordinances governing the use of fireworks in your community.

THANKSGIVING DINNER

There are few more warm and festive occasions than Thanksgiving. If you're planning a big Thanksgiving dinner for a large group of family and friends, you should extend invitations well in advance—from four weeks to two months earlier—since many of the celebrants are likely to be traveling from a distance away and need to make plans ahead of time. Guests should respond to the invitations as soon as possible.

Thanksgiving meals require much preparation, particularly if your guest list contains more than six people. If you are preparing a meal for more than 10 people, it's fine to ask other guests to help out by bringing certain parts of the meal. Enlist the help of family members in all Thanksgiving chores. You'll want to tap someone to carve the turkey a few minutes before the meal is to begin.

The fellowship feeling of Thanksgiving is unrivaled among holidays. That's why it's a wonderful time to extend a last-minute invitation to someone who may be alone or without plans for the holidays. It's a good time, too, to contribute canned goods or money to volunteer organizations that feed the homeless, the elderly, and the infirm.

CHAPTER 7

ENTERTAINING OUTSIDE THE HOME

RESTAURANTS AND CLUBS

Hosting a party in a restaurant or country club makes sense for several reasons—if your space at home is too small to accommodate a large guest list, for example, or you don't want to deal with the fuss of preparing and serving food and cleaning up afterward. A favorite restaurant is also a festive place for a celebration. In either case, if mistakes occur, the host must tactfully and politely see that they are corrected, without embarrassing the guests.

The thoughtful host first considers the choice of restaurant. Do the guests like exotic food or home-style cooking? If they are from out of town, would they like to see a place that is widely known or one with a good local reputation? If a man is taking a woman to dinner, he might consider whether she prefers a small, intimate spot or a hot dance club. Perhaps you will want to offer your guests a choice of a few suggested restaurants. It all depends on your guests' preferences and your own insiders' knowledge. It's a good idea to try the restaurant yourself before inviting others to be your guests there.

Always reserve a table at a well-known restaurant ahead of time; if you are planning a large party, it goes without saying that you must make a reservation and make food selections in advance. Be sure to arrive before your guests so that they don't have to stand and wait in the restaurant lobby for any period of time.

When one couple invites another to dine, the host and hostess generally sit opposite one another. In larger groups, the guest of honor is seated to the host's or hostess's right with men and women alternating around the table. Ordinarily, a couple does not sit next to each other; this gives people a chance to socialize with others.

ORDERING DRINKS

If a guest refuses the offer of a predinner cocktail, a host should not push him or her to accept. On the other hand, no guest should feel uncomfortable requesting a drink when the host does not. To ensure that his guests feel comfortable doing so, the host could say something like, "I don't think I'll have a cocktail, but please go ahead—I'll have mineral water while you're having your gin and tonic." It is impolite, however, to order more than one or two cocktails when others are left with nothing in front of them and only the hope of a meal to sustain them.

If your party decides to drink wine with dinner, it's a good idea to order the wine after the choices for the meal have been made. Then the person best qualified should choose a wine that goes well with the greatest number of food selections. For instance, if more people have ordered chicken or fish, a white wine may be the best choice; but if more are having a steak dinner, a red may be preferred. Or a bottle of each may be ordered. Most restaurants also offer wine by the glass, which solves the problem of two people dining together who want different wines.

If you have a definite preference for red or white wine it is not incorrect to order either with any food. The choices stated above are simply those that, for the majority, result in the most pleasing combination of flavors.

If you don't recognize the names on the wine list, by all means ask your waiter's advice, giving him an idea of the types of wine you prefer.

ORDERING THE MEAL

For many years the rule was that the woman told the man what she would like and he gave the order—she never so much as spoke to the waiter herself. Today, of course, this custom seems ridiculous and outdated. When a couple is dining in a restaurant alone, the man may graciously relay his date's menu request if this is what he and she prefer. But when more than two people are dining out, there is no reason why the women can't give the waiter their own orders. It is certainly less confusing to do it that way, especially if the group is large. When the waiter looks straight at a woman and asks, "What kind of dressing would you like?" it is confusing and insulting if she turns away and relays her message through her escort. In fact, many waiters ask the woman for her order first in an effort to be polite—and there is no reason why she shouldn't offer a direct response.

When one member of the party knows the restaurant and its specialties well or when exotic food is offered, the person who is most knowledgeable should suggest some choices. If all are unfamiliar with the type of food served, there should be no hesitation about asking the waiter for recommendations.

A guest should always show some consideration for the host's wallet by not ordering the most expensive items on the menu. Neither should a guest order the cheapest item, implying that he or she thinks the host can't afford more. For his part, the host can relay a message to his guest that no expense shall be spared or that guests are expected to order not just an entrée but appetizer, soup, and a salad course. He can do this by saying something like, "The filet mignon is excellent here—why don't you try it?" or "I'm having the special appetizer and a salad. What would you like to start with?"

A few very exclusive restaurants offer menus that show no prices. Presumably, if the host has chosen the restaurant, he is prepared to pay for whatever the guest selects. Although many guests may feel uncomfortable when this occurs, there is little to do except order what you like. If, however, you suspect the host or hostess had not realized that the restaurant made a practice of doing this, you can select an item that is ordinarily lower priced—a chicken dish instead of filet mignon, for example. If you are paying for your own meal, and a waiter or waitress recites a list of daily specials without mentioning the prices, you are perfectly correct in asking the cost of each item. If you are someone's guest, however, doing so might embarrass your host. It is up to the host to ask—or to suffer the consequences.

When the check comes, the host does not display the total but puts the money (or the signed form if paying by credit card) on the plate and subtly nods to the waiter to remove it.

GUESTS AT A PRIVATE CLUB

When you are invited to someone's private club, be sure to ask your host what you should wear, as many clubs have strict dress codes. If you're too shy to ask, simply call the club's office and ask about the dress code. In the same vein, it is never presumptuous for the host to mention the type of dress that is required at his club when he extends the invitation. Guests who are not aware of the customs of the club will be grateful for the information; showing up completely over- or underdressed could end up embarrassing both of you.

If you are invited by a friend to use his club facilities, such as the swimming pool or the golf course, offer to pay any guest fees up front.

Either way, any invitation to a private club is due a thank you—whether verbal or by note—and a follow-up invitation. If you yourself don't belong to a club, you can reciprocate by having your friends to dinner at home or in a restaurant, or inviting them to an outing such as the theater or a baseball game.

PERFORMANCES, CONCERTS, AND MOVIES

A fun way to entertain is to take friends out to the theater, a movie, a concert, or a ball game. If a friend suggests that a group of you go to the movies together, make sure you decide up front who's paying for the tickets—it's generally every man for himself. That way, you won't end up fighting over who's paying at the box-office window.

When you are invited to, say, the ballet or the theater, it is a nice gesture to offer to pay for dinner before or after. When you are offered a free ticket, you should still always offer to compensate the giver. If a friend has baseball season tickets and offers you a ticket when he is unable to attend a game, you should still say, "Can I pay you for this?" If the answer is no, you should always thank the person in some way, whether with a simple phone call the next day, an invitation to lunch, or a small gift or souvenir from the game.

THE GREAT OUTDOORS

Fast growing in popularity are invitations to share in an outdoor activity, whether a pool party, a ski weekend, a sailing excursion, or a round of golf at a country club. And just because your sailing skills, for example, may be rusty or even nonexistent, that doesn't mean you should refuse an invitation to go sailing. Simply explain to the hosts that you'd love to come, but you're not much of a sailor. If that doesn't matter, find out what you need to wear or bring—and have fun. People love to introduce newcomers to their favorite sports. Remember that good manners are still the rule, whether you're celebrating indoors or out.

POOL PARTIES

As anyone who has one can tell you, the luxury of a swimming pool in the back-yard has obligations attached beyond that of pool upkeep. Swimmers flock to a cool pool, and the pool owner often ends up entertaining friends and neighbors all summer long.

Pools are great fun to have, but you must stand firm in some ways or thoughtless neighbors will immediately impose on you. One solution to the problem of neighborhood children and adults dropping in to swim is to install a small flagpole at the gate to the pool. Inform friends and neighbors that they are invited to swim whenever the flag is raised. It will also mean that an adult will be there to supervise. When you have guests, or simply want the pool to yourselves, keep the flag down—and the neighborhood will know the pool is off limits.

If you are invited to enjoy a friend's pool, you should:

1. **BRING YOUR OWN TOWELS** Most hosts and hostesses keep a supply on hand, as well as an extra swimsuit or two, but the work of laundering and providing towels for guests can be extensive.

2. **BRING YOUR OWN BEVERAGES AND SNACKS** Pool owners who find that they are providing refreshments as well as swimming privileges to the neighborhood on a regular basis should tell their guests that they cannot go on providing snacks and drinks. Return the hospitality of a pool-owning friend by bringing sandwiches for the group and offering to buy soft drinks, beer, or iced tea.

3. **HELP SUPERVISE WHEN YOUR CHILDREN ARE INVITED OVER TO SWIM** Children's pool parties—even those of teens—should have adult supervision. Water accidents do happen, and few children are equipped to handle them competently.

SKI WEEKENDS: A GUEST'S GUIDE

With the rising popularity of winter sports, more and more people are acquiring lodges or condominiums in the mountains, and ski weekends are becoming practically an institution in some sections of the country. When invited to be someone's guest for a weekend of skiing, you are a houseguest, and as such will follow the guidelines for being a gracious one. If you don't ski and have no desire to learn, simply say so. If you welcome the opportunity to get away and would be content to spend your time reading, exploring the area, and entertaining yourself, make that known up front so that your host doesn't feel obligated to stay home with you and miss prime skiing time.

If, on the other hand, you do ski or would like to learn but have no equipment, you cannot expect your host to supply it. Either rent the equipment from a store or ask your host if rentals are available at the slopes. Insist on paying for your own rentals as well as the cost of your lift tickets. Your host is providing lodging and hospitality but is certainly not obliged to pay the considerable costs associated with skiing for his houseguests.

And you should not ask to use the host's other equipment, such as a snowmobile, unless he offers the use of it to you. Be sure to get a lesson before you drive away.

SKI WEEKENDS: A HOST'S GUIDE

As the host, you should make the details of the arrangements known to guests when issuing the invitation. These details include a basic schedule as well as expected costs for equipment and lift tickets. The uninitiated may be unaware of the costs involved, and courtesy requires that the host make them known before expecting a response to the invitation. You should also mention wardrobe needs—whether simply casual outfits and snow-weather gear or a dressy getup or two. Many ski resorts and condos have hot tubs; let guests know beforehand so that they may pack swimming suits.

CHAPTER 8

BUSINESS ENTERTAINING

These days, business and social life overlap in innumerable ways. For many people, work life is the wellspring from which social life develops. This often makes it hard to know when to separate the two. Because business and play have become increasingly interwoven, it is imperative that workers maintain a clear sense of where one ends and the other begins.

Socializing with business associates does offer a great opportunity to talk in a relaxed atmosphere, to cement relationships, and to get to know clients, employers, and employees better. Combining meals with business ensures that the flow of work continues uninterrupted during the work day.

Being relaxed, however, does not mean that business relationships become intimate or personal just because you are outside the office setting. Just as your appearance, behavior, and manners are used in the office as criteria for your promotability, so are they used outside the office too. Having too much to drink, being loud or rude, and even dressing inappropriately can be strikes against you in the eyes of your employers. And if you are the boss, it goes without saying that your professional image must be intact no matter what the social situation.

ENTERTAINING OUTSIDE THE OFFICE
RESTAURANT BUSINESS MEALS

Sometimes there just aren't enough hours in the business day to get everything done without including breakfast, lunch, and dinner in the schedule. If your workday spills over into lunch or dinner, here are a few pointers keep in mind.

- When the invitation is yours, you can either ask your guest's choice of restaurants or give him a choice between two or three options. If he defers to your good judgment, select a restaurant that is close to your guest's office or centrally located to both of you. Pick a restaurant with a low noise level and one where tables are spaced far enough apart to ensure privacy.

- Make a reservation. Wasting time waiting in line just to be seated is just that—wasting time. Make every effort to arrive early, before your guest.
- If you are the guest and you are the first to arrive, you may be shown to your table if there is a reservation—especially if the restaurant is full or filling up. Or you can wait in the foyer of the restaurant for your host to arrive.
- Whether you are the host or the guest, you should stand to greet your party when they arrive.

- Seat your guest in the preferred seat, generally the one that looks out at a view or into the restaurant.
- Both the host and guest should order food that can be eaten easily while talking between bites. This is much more important than it sounds. Wrestling with a lobster (not to mention wearing a lobster bib!) may make you look more foolish than professional.
- If you're having lunch, it's better not to drink alcohol. If you must, keep it to one drink. Business dining means business will be conducted, and you need your wits about you. If you're drinking at dinner, the same is true: don't overdo it.
- As host, you should indicate to your guest that he or she is welcome to order freely and without concern for cost by recommending something from the menu at the more expensive end of the price range. Or you can tell him what you will be having and even suggest he also choose an appetizer, clueing in your guest on how to order. If you are the guest, on the other hand, that doesn't mean you have the green light to run up the tab—always exercise restraint.
- Time is precious: Be aware of your party's other obligations.
- If you are the guest, do not attempt to snatch the check—the host pays. Only when two coworkers, at any level, agree to meet for lunch is the check split between them. Otherwise, it is assumed that the one inviting a guest is also the one who pays the check. The host pays as well for checking the guest's coat.

Breakfast Meetings. Breakfast meetings are a great way for morning people who think best over a cup of coffee and breakfast to start the day. Again, meetings should be held at a mutually convenient location and should be kept relatively short, since all concerned still have to get to the office. Breakfast meetings are particularly efficient when your professional agenda is short and your days are jam-packed with other meetings.

Dinner Invitations. Business dinner invitations are less common than lunches since they obviously impinge on people's personal, out-of-the-office time. However, when executives are so busy that they cannot meet for lunch—or when there might be a special occasion to be handled over dinner—a business dinner may be arranged. A dinner invitation usually includes a group of people brought together for a common purpose.

Business dinner invitations should be extended well in advance. An executive's assistant may either telephone guests or write them a note saying "Mr. Franklin would like to take Mr. Jones to dinner on the 27th," for example. Those without assistants make the invitations themselves in the same way. The invitation should be addressed to the businessperson only, at his office, so it is clear that the dinner is a business-related one and that spouses are not included. A reservation should be made at a convenient restaurant, at a quiet table or in a private room.

You as host must be there ahead of time to greet your guests, introduce them if they are not acquainted, and seat them at a table. Place the highest-ranking guest or the one due the greatest honor at your right; the second highest, at your left. Others you may seat at random. If everyone is on the same level, you might simply suggest that people sit anywhere they please.

You should order drinks when everyone arrives; if, however, someone is late, order anyway and let the latecomer catch up upon arrival. One or two predinner drinks is often the average. When you order wine with dinner, it is wise to have a bottle of red and one of white.

TICKETS TO THE SHOW

Entertaining clients or business associates isn't restricted to meals. Many businesspeople entertain with tickets to a special event, such as the theater, a jazz club, or a baseball game, and plan dinner or lunch around that event. When in New York, for example, clients who are theater buffs may be taken to a top

Broadway show; while in New Orleans, jazz lovers are often treated to an evening out in the French Quarter.

CLUB ENTERTAINING

One of the traditional ways businessmen—and women—have entertained clients is at the golf club or country club. This may include a round of golf or a few sets of tennis. More major decisions are made, it is said, on the 17th hole than in the executive office.

When you do this kind of entertaining, you may meet at the club in the morning, play golf or tennis, eat lunch, and then part, either to return to work or to go home. On the other hand, you may both work in the morning, drive to the club—together or separately—for lunch, and then spend the afternoon together on the links or on the court. Either scenario provides an enjoyable and effective way to entertain for business.

ENTERTAINING IN THE OFFICE

CORPORATE DINING-ROOM ENTERTAINING

Employees of corporations and large companies often entertain in a corporate dining room on the office premises. The only differences between entertaining a guest at a restaurant and in the executive dining room are that menu choices are often limited—and there is no check at the end of the meal.

If the menu is preset, the host should ask his or her guests if they have any food preferences when extending the invitation. The host should be present to greet guests, take their coats, and direct them to restrooms.

When a group is being entertained, seating protocol is important. The most important guest sits on the host's right and the second most important on the host's left. If there is a second host, she sits opposite the host, with the third and fourth most-important guests to her right and left.

The host is responsible for conversation and for introducing the agenda at the appropriate time. He is also responsible for keeping conversation on the agenda once the business discussion begins.

It is up to the host to end the lunch by placing his napkin on the table and rising, once he is certain everyone is finished and that the business discussion is concluded.

The host sees guests out, retrieving their coats and directing them to the elevator or stairs.

ENTERTAINING WITH SPOUSES AND PARTNERS

Most parties held at the office or during the work day do not include spouses or dates. Some occasions, however, do call for including spouses. They are:

- When out-of-town businesspeople and their spouses or partners visit in your area;
- When you return an invitation that included your spouse;
- When you want to get to know your client better;
- When the occasion to which you are extending the invitation is a couple's affair, such as a formal dinner or a dance;
- When you and a business associate find you have become friends and want to enjoy and share that friendship with your spouses;
- When you, as boss, wish to get to know your employees personally and have them know you as a person as well.

When you extend an invitation that includes spouses and partners, include your own; when you accept, accept for both of you. If you are the host but are unattached, invite a date; when you are a guest invited to a couple's event, you may ask if you can bring a friend. Couples who are unmarried but who live together should be treated exactly the same as married couples. Any party, whether at the office or at a private home, to which husbands and wives are invited should properly include any live-in partners. There are, of course, office parties to which spouses are not invited. Live-in partners should not be expected to attend those either.

If your partner has been excluded from an invitation because of the host's ignorance of your arrangement, just ask, "May I bring Kathleen Jennings, the woman I live with?" or, "I live with Bill Adams, and I'd like to bring him. Is that all right?" Since good manners dictate that a live-in partner be invited to social occasions just as a spouse is, the answer should be affirmative. If the reply is negative, however, you must decide whether you want to attend the affair alone or decline the invitation altogether. If it's the latter, you may politely explain, "I'm sorry, then, but I won't be able to accept. Thank you for inviting me all the same."

ENTERTAINING AT HOME

Home entertaining goes a step beyond outside entertaining. Business associates feel like friends when they share the relaxed atmosphere of someone's personal surroundings. When people invite business associates and clients to their homes, spouses are automatically included. Occasionally, a breakfast or lunch for business associates is held in someone's private home, but at those times the venue is generally chosen for convenience and privacy rather than a social occasion.

If you are not married but are living with someone, your partner is treated the same as a spouse would be. Even though business associates may not know you live with someone, it is your choice to tell them or not. If you are the host, a simple introduction of your partner is all that is needed as guests arrive.

The challenge to inviting a few business associates to your home is to do so without offending others at the office. Either invite those you've left off the list another time or keep the invitation private. Some employers make a ritual of inviting each member of their staff once during the year; some throw parties with small groups, and others invite the entire staff at once. What you do depends on the accommodations your home can provide and the kind of entertaining that you and your spouse prefer.

One of the warmest ways to entertain business associates is to include one or two with nonbusiness friends in your home. In this way you truly make your coworkers feel like personal friends.

Greeting Guests

If couples arrive and you haven't met your business associate's spouse, greet your coworker first with a handshake. Then quickly turn to his spouse (whose name you probably know at this point) and say something like "Hello, Susan. I'm so happy to meet you." Your own spouse should be close behind you as you greet them so that you may turn and say, "I'd like you to meet my wife [or husband]. Jennifer [or Michael]; this is Eric Appleton and his wife, Susan."

At a small party, the host should then take his guests around the room, introducing them to people they do not know. In a large gathering, such as a cocktail party, business associates may assume this responsibility themselves, introducing their own spouses to their coworkers.

The Role of Your Spouse or Partner

Your spouse, your home, and your entertaining style all reflect who you are and the choices you've made, and for better or worse, leave an indelible impression on those you work with every day. When you entertain at home, your spouse or partner is there to support you—to make your guests feel welcome, to help them enjoy being with you both, as well as to assist with refreshments. Since there will undoubtedly be a great deal of shop talk, it is your spouse's role to be interested—to listen, to ask questions, to indicate the involvement of both of you in the company. At the same time, your husband or wife should feel free to discuss his or her profession and personal interests.

The Single Host or Hostess

If you are single and inviting business associates into your home, it's a smart idea to ask a friend to help you host the party. While it is by no means a requirement for a single person to have a stand-in host or hostess, it does make entertaining easier. Business entertaining at home is different from purely social entertaining in that a portion of the guests (the business associates) know each other well, while the rest of the crowd (generally spouses or dates) may not know each other at all. Having two hosts on duty eases the workload and allows the single host to give equal attention to spouses and dates.

When a single woman gives a business party, she may ask a close friend to act as host. One responsibility of the stand-in host may be to handle drinks—to either serve them or see that guests are attended to by waiters or at a self-service bar. Another responsibility is to talk with guests, particularly with the spouses, who may feel out of place. Although the hostess will also be circulating to speak with guests, she may be busy making last-minute preparations and serving hors d'oeuvres or dinner.

The same logic applies when a single man hosts a business party. Similarly, it's a good idea to enlist a friend to help out. While the responsibility for food and drinks will fall upon him, his cohost can help by engaging his business associates and helping spouses and dates become acquainted.

A Word of Caution

Since home entertaining merges your business and social lives, exert caution when undertaking it. If, as an upper-management executive, you socialize regularly with your staff, there is a chance that you may weaken your position of authority, making it difficult to reprimand or fire someone or to pass over someone for a raise or a promotion. If you socialize with your boss and your coworkers do not, you may create resentment among the rest of the staff and be accused of deliberately currying favor. Home entertainment on a regular basis should be confined to peers or clients who have become friends. The occasional home party may include anyone in the office.

ENTERTAINING THE BOSS

Inviting the boss to lunch or dinner can be a tricky proposition. You may invite a coworker, a client, a prospective client, a peer from another company, and—from time to time—your secretary or assistant, to breakfast, lunch, or dinner during the business week. If you are the boss, you may invite any members of your staff and colleagues from another company. But it's not a good idea to invite a superior to a restaurant during the business day. Rare exceptions: if you've worked with your boss for many years or are old friends who knew each other before you worked together.

If someone in a superior position invites you or you and your spouse or live-in partner to a *social* occasion, however, you are expected to return the invitation in some way. The following are a few guidelines that may lessen the dilemma:

- In general, an invitation extended in person is proper for coworkers, but a boss should get a written invitation. Write the invitation to your boss and his or her spouse.
- If you call your boss "Mr." or "Ms." at the office, don't suddenly switch to "Bob" or "Betty" either in the invitation or as you speak during the evening—that is, unless your boss suggests it. If you call your boss by title and last name, your spouse should follow suit. If you and your spouse address your boss by title and last name, you should both address his or her spouse similarly.
- You may find it easier to entertain your boss if you include a few other guests. Select people with similar interests.
- You need not reciprocate your boss's invitation in kind. For instance, you may repay a fancy dinner at a restaurant with a simple buffet dinner in your home.
- Finally, don't put on airs when you entertain the boss. Act as you normally act; entertain as you normally entertain. Do not hire special help unless you ordinarily do; do not serve a hard-to-carve roast unless you can handle it. In other

words, be yourself and be comfortable. Being gracious and interested will impress the boss far more than outdoing yourself in a way that he, above all, knows you cannot afford.

WEEKEND ENTERTAINING

If you own a country place, you may wish to extend an invitation for the weekend to business associates or clients and their spouses. Unless you and your spouse know them well, however, and feel comfortable with them, a weekend can create tension, for there is no escape. A weekend is easier if you have a large place with facilities for such activities as swimming, boating, skiing, or tennis. If you do not have domestic help, you should prepare as much as possible ahead of time, since a host relegated to the kitchen all day can do little to add to the guests' comfort. Planned evenings add pleasure to weekend entertaining: a country auction, a summer-stock play, outdoor music, or a local fair is often available nearby.

WEDDINGS

Keep in mind that weddings should never be used as an opportunity to pay off business obligations or to sell or promote a business deal. Some business executives do use the occasion of a large wedding to entertain clients, prospective clients, and business associates. First, if the wedding is that of a son or daughter, do this only with his or her approval—even if you are paying for the entire wedding. Second, be careful not to slight anyone by failure to extend an invitation. Naturally, you would invite business associates who are also friends without having to invite the entire department or your complete client list.

OFFICE PARTIES

The days of office parties where coworkers let down their hair, got roaring drunk, and ended up with lampshades on their heads are almost over and gone. Today, fortunately, the office party has matured, by and large, into a more relaxing, morale-building time of good cheer and camaraderie.

INVITATIONS

Invitations to office parties are more informal than those for social affairs. The host may send a memo on paper or by e-mail to each staff member. It might read something like: "The graphic services department will celebrate a good year and a merry Christmas on Friday, December 23, in the office. All work stops at 3:30 P.M. sharp for cocktails and a buffet. I look forward to celebrating with you." When an office party is held in a restaurant rather than in the office, invitations may sometimes be more formal—on cards, handwritten for small groups, printed for large ones.

Details of party arrangements—generally, the food and drinks—are often delegated to staff members. Some offices plan entertainment, whether music, gift-giving, or a sports-related activity.

THE HOLIDAY PARTY

A holiday party held during the Christmas season is usually hosted by the company. In a larger company, the heads of individual departments may host parties for their own staffs. If the department head is away or so antisocial as to eschew parties, a lower-level executive may host the party instead. In rare cases the staff throws its own party.

Spouses and dates may or may not be invited. At office parties held at a restaurant, the host generally stands by the door and greets each staff member upon arrival. In the office the host circulates, shaking hands and greeting the staff with a personal word of thanks.

OFFICE PARTY DRESS

At a party held in the workplace, both men and women generally just show up in the clothes they have worn all day. Or, they may have brought along or worn fancier dress than usual that morning in anticipation of the event. Although overdressing—not to mention underdressing—is generally out of place, many women like to dress up their office wear with jewelry or other accessories.

At an office party held outside the office, both men and women may properly change from work clothes into dress clothes. Still, because it is a business affair, overly dressy or revealing clothing is in poor taste.

People who drink too much at office parties are taking the risk of seriously harming their professional careers. Sloppiness and a lack of self-control become obvious to superiors, who will think twice—or not at all—about giving big drinkers future responsibilities. The unruly also create embarrassing situations for themselves and their associates, whom they have to face at work again. A good host keeps a careful eye on his staff during an office party; if he sees people overdrinking, he should quietly steer them away from the bar. If they fail to get the hint and return for another, he may say—gently—in private, "I think you've had enough to drink, don't you? Why don't you get something to eat and a cup of coffee?"

Equally disadvantageous is the practice of becoming too intimate at office parties. With too much to drink and in the spirit of seasonal abandon, men and women often place themselves in regrettable situations. Personal secrets may be exchanged and amorous overtures made and accepted, which may seem less than romantic in the clear light of the office workday. The safest way to avoid such embarrassment is to be aware of its possibility and stay in control. Limiting your drinking is a starting point.

Don't forget that even a peck on the cheek can be misconstrued by coworkers. Kissing has no place in business surroundings among people who barely know one another or who see one another all the time. A kiss is not a casual greeting but an indication of real affection. If a boss has been away for a while and greets his employees in a social setting, he might be justified in a "hello" kiss. Otherwise, when he is working with them regularly, there is no justification for that kind of greeting—not even socially.

For years the occasional drunk was the most visible sign of overindulgence at an office party. Today, however, a radical change in behavior could be due to the use of drugs. Those who choose to use drugs may believe they are no worse than alcohol. But the fact is that alcohol is legal, and, so far, drugs are not. It should go without saying: The use of any illegal substance will not be tolerated. If the host of the office party witnesses the use of drugs, the offender should be asked to leave.

Groups of people at an office party often want to extend the festivities after the party is over, going to someone's house or to a local bar to drink and dance. This can be fun if warnings about overdrinking and intimacy are heeded. Attention must also be given to transportation home. Plans should be made ahead of time for people to travel together whenever possible. If someone commutes to work from out of town, he or she might be able to arrange to sleep over at a coworker's home.

OTHER OFFICE OCCASIONS

Many offices have parties for occasions other than Christmas: when someone leaves or retires; when someone is going to be married or is having a baby; or when someone achieves an outstanding honor. Office sports teams often celebrate sporting events with postgame get-togethers.

Special-occasion parties may be given by the boss or by the staff and should include the entire department and any special friends the guest of honor may have in other areas of the company. While spouses are not necessarily included, the spouse of the guest of honor is often invited to share the occasion.

An informal party may be given in the office, or a lunch or dinner is planned at a nearby restaurant. A staff committee may be appointed to handle such details as time, place, menu, and gifts. Bills should be given directly to the boss if he or she is hosting the party; they should be split among the staff if they are the hosts.

RETURNING AN INVITATION

Business invitations need not be returned in the same way that social invitations must be. You do not return a business lunch or dinner invitation from your boss, but you do return, in some form, a social invitation. If, as a client, a salesperson or supplier invites you or entertains you, you are not expected to repay this business lunch or dinner, although you certainly may if you have continuing business together. Neither are you expected to repay a social invitation where you, as a client, have been entertained, even if the invitation has included your spouse or your entire family. You are, however, expected to return social invitations from coworkers and other business associates, whether they have extended a hand of friendship to cement a business relationship or simply because you enjoy one another's company outside the office.

THANK-YOU GIFTS AND NOTES

When you have been entertained at a business-related occasion that crosses from business to social—whether at a dinner, an evening out with your spouse, at a weekend house party at the home of an employer, or as guest of honor at an office party—a thank-you note is in order. When you are one of many guests at an office party or a restaurant where you share a meal in the ordinary course of business, a verbal thanks at the end of the occasion is sufficient. While it is never wrong to write a thank-you note, you may reiterate your thanks in your next business correspondence in place of a separate thank you.

When the occasion is a social one, your thank-you note should be addressed to your host and his or her spouse and sent to their home. Social thank-you notes are handwritten on informal or personal stationery.

Business-occasion thank-you notes come in several varieties. If your company honors you with a dinner celebrating your 25 years with the firm, for example, a handwritten note on personal stationery is called for; it is addressed to your immediate boss, and to the president of the company if he or she attended the gathering.

If you, as the client, have been a lunch guest, a thank-you note is called for. But if you speak to your host often, a verbal thanks is sufficient. If you are the lunch guest of a client you see regularly, a separate note of thanks is not necessary. You would, instead, mention your thanks for the lunch in your next letter, "Thanks again, Jim, for joining me at lunch [or 'for lunch' if your client treated]. We really accomplished a lot. I'll have that proposal to you by next week."

When a business lunch is a first meeting or an infrequent one, a short note is in order, whether typed by your secretary on business letterhead or handwritten by you.

CHAPTER 9

CELEBRATION RITUALS

The markers or milestones of a lifetime are often the traditional celebrations of special days, whether birthdays, holidays, or anniversaries. Entertaining on these occasions can result in the most congenial and memorable events of a lifetime.

ANNIVERSARY PARTIES

Anniversary parties can be given in honor of any anniversary, but the "big ones," the ones most often celebrated, are the first, fifth, 10th, 25th, and 50th. Parties given for the first three are usually informal and indistinguishable from any other reception except that guests toast the bride and groom and close friends bring gifts. A couple may celebrate any anniversary as they wish. For the 25th and 50th anniversaries, certain customs are generally followed. Some couples who marry late in life may feel that they will never reach their golden anniversary and wonder whether having a big celebration on their 35th or 40th is proper. Of course it is!

When it is convenient the party is held on the actual date of the anniversary, but it is perfectly fine to move it forward or back a few days. If the husband or wife is ill or absent at the time, an anniversary may be celebrated several weeks after the true date. When the illness or the absence is prolonged, it is preferable to celebrate the anniversary the following year.

PLANNING THE PARTY

Early anniversary parties are generally given by the couple themselves. By the time the 25th anniversary rolls around, a couple may have grown children who want to make the arrangements. Even so, it is perfectly correct for the couple to throw the party themselves. When the celebrants have no children, close friends sometimes prepare the celebration. Fiftieth-anniversary celebrations are usually planned by the celebrants' family.

The party may be held just about anywhere: in the home of the couple, in the home of the person planning the party, in a church parish house, or in a room of a hotel, restaurant, or club.

If the party is a dinner or a small reception, the guest list is generally limited to family, members of the wedding party, and close friends. If it is to be a large reception or an open house, the list may include work associates and church, temple, or club members. In small close-knit communities, the guest list often includes everybody in town.

Decorations need not be elaborate. For the 25th anniversary party, white and silver ornaments and flowers are a nice touch; for the 50th, gold (or yellow) and white. Flowers make the loveliest decoration of all, and the "bride" should always be presented with a corsage.

Entertainment at an anniversary party is optional, but a strolling musician or a pianist adds a touch of romance. Ask the musician to play the couple's favorite tunes and any wedding music. If the host and hostess wish to hire an orchestra or provide records, dancing will be all the entertainment necessary.

PARTY REFRESHMENTS

The refreshments depend on the type of party being given—whether a luncheon, dinner, cocktail party, open house, or afternoon tea—and the level of formality. A fun idea for a 25th or 50th anniversary is a meal that replicates the one served at the couple's original wedding reception.

The only food that generally shows up at every wedding anniversary—particularly one for a long-married couple—is a wedding cake, which is cut and passed around with glasses of champagne for toasting the couple. A glass of champagne is the traditional drink for toasts—at any hour of the afternoon or evening. Otherwise the toasts may be made with punch or whatever drinks are available.

Other drinks at the party may range from tea and coffee at an afternoon reception to wine, champagne, or mixed drinks at an evening affair. Soft drinks should always be available for those who prefer them. Punch made with or without liquor is often served at open houses and other daytime parties.

THE PARTY

When the anniversary party is large, it's a good idea to have a receiving line. The couple usually stands near the door and greets their guests. Their children may join them in the line or, if the party is given by someone else, that person always heads the line as hostess. Older couples, who may tire easily or who may be unwell, can be seated in a central spot. That allows the guests, after greeting the hostess near the door, to move on to the honored pair and offer their congratulations.

If the party is a sit-down dinner, the table can be much like the bridal table at a wedding reception. The "bride and groom" sit together at the center of a long table or in the places facing the guests if the table is a round one. Any bridesmaids and ushers present are seated next to them; their husbands or wives are also included at the table. The couple's children are seated with them.

OPENING GIFTS

When gifts are brought to the anniversary couple—unless a "no gifts, please" was written on the invitation—the opening of the packages is often the party's main event unless the party is large or a dinner dance. After everyone has arrived or after dinner while the guests are enjoying their coffee, the group gathers round and the couple opens the gifts.

PICTURES

Because an anniversary party is often the kind of memorable occasion that brings together friends and relatives from afar, make sure at least one person is taking photographs of the event. A professional photographer may even be hired for the party. These pictures, put into an attractive photo album, make a wonderful gift for the anniversary couple. A picture of the entire family, including children and grandchildren, also makes a perfect gift.

BABY SHOWERS

Generally, baby showers are given before the baby is born—unless the future mother requests that it be held after the baby is a few weeks old. Having the shower before the baby is born lets the mother-to-be ascertain what is left to purchase or borrow herself. It also adds excitement to the last weeks of a pregnancy. Some people, however, feel that baby showers are best given after the happy event takes place, because there is always a chance that something can go wrong. Indeed, nothing could be sadder for the bereaved mother and father than to have to return unused shower gifts.

At one time, mothers and sisters of the mother-to-be did not host a shower. That is no longer true, and these days, men are often being included in the festivities.

PLANNING THE PARTY

Invitations to baby showers may be sent up to six weeks before the shower. They should include the mother's name, the date and time of the shower, and a request for a response (R.S.V.P.). Sometimes it is a good idea to enclose directions to the hostess's house. An invitation to a baby shower should not include a list of items the mother-to-be needs, no matter how helpful the hostess feels this would be. Rather, she should be prepared with a list should an invited guest ask what is needed when responding to the invitation. At that time, she may also disclose the baby's sex, if she knows it, so that guests can buy accordingly.

Plans for the type of baby shower can range from simple and casual to elaborate. Naturally, the food menu is dictated by the time of day the shower is held. If the baby shower is to be held after dinner (often on a weekday) or during a weekend afternoon, the food should be light. But that doesn't mean it can't be elegant. In the evening, pair desserts with beverages like coffee, tea, fruit juices, or white or rosé wine. In the afternoon, light snacks, such as tea sandwiches, cookies, and petit fours, hit the spot. You might serve these snacks with cold fruit-juice punch, coffee, and iced tea.

The decor for a baby shower can also range from the simple to over the top. Always popular are flowers, balloons, streamers, and customized baby-shower paper goods found in party or stationery stores. Creative hostesses can carry the baby theme even further by decorating the table with colorful baby bottles filled with flowers (daisies or gerbera), by pinning napkins into diaper shapes with big diaper pins, or by using small teething rings as napkin holders and rattles as silverware rests.

Showers may be given for second babies, but they should be restricted to either very close friends and family or to people who were not invited to showers for the first baby. They are appropriate if the mother has moved to a new area and has a new circle of friends or if a number of years have passed since the first baby's birth. A baby shower held for a second child is fine, but it can become an imposition to ask the same people to a third or fourth baby shower. You are not obligated to accept these invitations nor to send a gift if you do not go. Simply refuse politely, and send the prospective or new parents a congratulatory card. If you decide to accept, you must of course, bring a gift.

It is not only correct but extremely thoughtful to give a shower for the mother or father of an adopted baby. It should be exactly the same as any baby shower, except that with the invitations you may want to include the correct size for baby clothes, if the child is not a newborn, or the baby's sex, if it is known. A shower may be given, as well, when the adopted child is not an infant but rather an older baby or even a toddler, since the celebration is for the arrival of the child as a new member of the family.

It is perfectly acceptable to give a small shower for an expectant single mother, or for one whose baby is already born. A single parent particularly needs the love and support of her family and friends, and the baby should be made as welcome to the world as those close to the mother can make him or her.

BIRTHDAY PARTIES FOR GROWN-UPS

Celebrating the "big" birthdays—whether 21 or 50 or 75—is a big deal these days. Maybe that's because people are living longer—or maybe it's that there are virtually no limits on the kind of celebration you can throw. A 40th birthday fete could be celebrated with a traditional cocktail party, a dinner party, or a "Come as You Were When Dave Was 30" party. A nice feature would be a toast—or many toasts—to the birthday person, which can even take the form of poems, songs, funny anecdotes, or tributes.

Invitations may be handwritten notes, store bought fill-in cards, or even telephone calls, depending on the formality of the event. Because it is a birthday party, it is assumed that gifts are to be brought, unless the invitation indicates "No gifts, please." The guest of honor may elect to open them after the

Celebration
Rituals

party, depending on the formality of the occasion and any other activities occurring.

COMING-OF-AGE PARTIES

As a child grows and matures, several milestone ceremonies commemorate his or her religious and academic achievement or simply celebrate a "landmark" age. Although it is not mandatory to have a party to mark each of these achievements, some recognition, if just a hug or a personal note, should be given.

Celebrants invited to religious services of other faiths do have some responsibilities. While it is not expected that you recite creeds, genuflect, or do anything that is contrary to your own faith, it is expected that you rise and sit when others do, and that you follow along and participate in all aspects of the service that are not contrary to your own beliefs.

FIRST COMMUNION

First Communion for a Catholic child takes place when the youngster is six or seven. It is the first occasion in which he or she actually receives the Host, and as such is an important event in the child's religious life. The child attends a course of instruction to learn both the meaning and the ritual, and the entire class receives First Communion together.

Although some families celebrate the occasion with elaborate festivities, most restrict the celebration to relatives and a few close friends who attend the service and, if they are also Catholic, participate in the mass. The little girls wear white dresses ranging from simple white costumes to more elaborate outfits with veils and headpieces. The boys wear dark suits with white shirts and ties.

Usually a small party is held for the young celebrant at the parents' home, or the family may go to his or her favorite restaurant for a dinner party. Immediate family members give meaningful gifts of a lasting nature.

For Protestant children, First Communion takes place at an older age, usually between 11 and 14, depending on the denomination. Girls generally wear nice dresses, and boys wear shirts and slacks with or without a jacket and tie. Most often, the ceremony is held during a regular church service with the entire congregation participating.

Celebrations are held at the discretion of the parents and gifts are given only by immediate family members, if at all. If guests are invited to a Communion party, then a gift is taken. Others may send cards if they wish to recognize this important event in a child's life.

CONFIRMATION

Confirmation is a religious occasion rather than a social one. It is the moment when the young person confirms the vows that were made for him or her by parents and godparents at the time of baptism. It is a thoughtful and serious event and therefore is celebrated joyfully—but with restraint.

Catholic children are generally confirmed when they are 11 or 12; Protestants, a year or two older. A confirmation may be done at any age, and there is a special confirmation for those who change their faith.

The candidates for confirmation in all faiths undergo a period of instruction. Those who complete these lessons satisfactorily are confirmed by the church minister, a bishop, or another high church dignitary in the manner of a graduating class. The service in the Protestant Church is usually held at a regular Sunday service. In the Catholic Church, it is separate from the regular mass, attended by members of the families and close friends of the young people.

Some churches hold an informal reception after the ceremony, and anyone in the congregation may attend. Afterward, the family and a few friends may gather at the parents' home for lunch, and those who wish give the newly confirmed youngster a gift, often of a religious nature—a Bible with his or her name engraved on it, a prayer book, or a gold cross.

Catholic girls wear white dresses and sometimes a short veil. Some Protestant ministers request that the girls wear white, but most ask only that they wear simple, modest dresses in quiet colors. This is up to the discretion of the minister. In both Protestant and Catholic churches, the boys wear dark blue or dark gray suits or jackets and ties with nice slacks.

BAR MITZVAH

A Jewish boy's bar mitzvah or confirmation celebrates his acceptance as an adult member of his congregation. In the Orthodox and Conservative branches, and in some Reform congregations, the bar mitzvah takes place on the first Sabbath (Saturday) after the boy turns 13. Other Reform congregations have replaced the bar mitzvah with a confirmation service at which both boys and girls are confirmed, sometimes at an older age than the traditional 13. As in the Christian church, candidates have undergone a period of religious instruction prior to the ceremony.

In addition to being a deeply religious occasion, the bar mitzvah differs from the Christian confirmation in that it is always celebrated socially as well. It is one of the most important events in a boy's life, and the family generally makes every effort to make it as wonderful and celebratory an occasion as they can. The religious ceremony may be followed immediately by a gathering in the social rooms of the synagogue, and is followed after that by the party.

The bar mitzvah party—whether luncheon, dinner, or a reception—usually includes all the close friends of the parents as well as friends and classmates of the boy. Only those who receive invitations may attend.

Invitations may be engraved in third-person style if the party is formal; they may be handwritten notes or they may be telephoned if it is not. They must, like other invitations, be acknowledged promptly, and in kind.

The reception itself is just like any other. Dinners and luncheons may be sit-down or buffet, and the party may be held at home or in a club, hotel, or restaurant. A band is sometimes hired to provide background music and for dancing.

Guests at the ceremony wear the clothes that they ordinarily choose for a religious service, with men wearing yarmulkes on their heads for all but Reform congregations. If the celebration is later in the day, they may change into clothes more appropriate for an evening party. If the affair is formal or black tie, this should be specified on the invitation. Otherwise the women wear cocktail dresses or long skirts and the men wear dark suits. Everyone invited to a bar mitzvah is expected to give a gift, and the boy must, of course, write thank-you letters promptly for each and every one.

BAT MITZVAH

The bat mitzvah is a corresponding ceremony to a bar mitzvah for girls of 12 or 13 in some Conservative and Reform congregations. A tradition that began only in the twentieth century, bat mitzvah means "daughter of the commandment." The ceremony closely resembles the bar mitzvah ceremony for boys, with girls reading from the Torah, leading other parts of the service, and generally delivering a speech to the congregation on the importance of attaining religious adulthood. Like a bar mitzvah, a bat mitzvah is part of a larger service and is almost always held on a Saturday.

Guests should follow the practice of the synagogue during the service, with men wearing a yarmulke on their heads for all but some Reform congregations. Yarmulkes are available outside the sanctuary. Some Conservative synagogues also require that married women wear a hat or other form of head covering. When a tallith, or prayer shawl, is available at the entrance to the sanctuary, it is only for those of the Jewish faith. Out of courtesy for the members of the host congregation, non-Jews should neither pick up a tallith nor wear religious symbols of other faiths.

The reception may be as simple or as elaborate as the parents wish to make it. Invited guests are expected to send a gift if they must regret or to send one to the child's home or take one if they attend a reception. Gifts should not be taken to the religious ceremony. The bat mitzvah honoree must write a thank-you note for all gifts she receives.

QUINCEAÑERA

The celebration of a Latin American girl's 15th birthday, a *quinceañera,* often simply called a *quince,* can be either a party or a religious celebration followed by a party, depending on the practice of the Roman Catholic Church in the area. If a religious ceremony precedes the party, it may simply involve a blessing, or it may have lengthy requirements that include the reaffirmation of baptismal vows and/or a catechism class.

Not dissimilar in concept to a debutante ball, the celebration commemorates coming of age, or a young girl's passage into womanhood. A highlight of the party usually includes the tradition of the birthday girl waltzing with her father before general dancing begins. Very often the party is formal, with guests wearing either black or white tie, as noted on the invitation, and the young girl wearing an elaborate, formal gown.

Gifts are customary—either money or personal items, depending on the tradition of the area. The gifts are usually not opened during the party, which follows the form of a ball or dance rather than a traditional birthday celebration.

SWEET-16 PARTIES

A 16th birthday is a milestone. It represents the division between childhood and young adulthood. It is therefore often celebrated more elaborately than other birthdays. Although there is no rule about it, the sweet-16 party seems to be largely a female prerogative; few boys have 16th birthday parties. The venue is often home, although clubs and restaurants are sometimes rented out for the occasion.

A sweet-16 party is usually given by the girl's parents or other family members. It can be held as a planned party or a surprise. The form runs the gamut: from slumber parties to pizza parties to pool parties to formal dances.

Invitations may be telephoned, but when the celebration is more formal, they are usually written on decorated, fill-in commercial invitations that are specifically made for sweet-16 parties. For a mixed party a girl may send invitations to all her friends—boys and girls—or else invite only the girls and ask them to bring a date. If she knows the date's name she sends him an invitation too. All invitations should have "R.S.V.P." on them, followed by a telephone number. If your party is to be catered you must know the number of guests coming, so you may enclose a response card.

Gifts are expected at a sweet-16 party and are usually somewhat more elaborate than for other birthdays. Each person who receives an invitation should take a present, but when a girl invites a boy to go with her, she selects a gift to be presented from them both. Writing thank-you notes is a must for the honoree.

GRADUATION PARTIES

In many cases, graduation gifts are all that are needed to acknowledge the occasion, but sometimes a graduate's family will throw a party in his or her honor to celebrate the event. Send out invitations at least three weeks ahead in case other members of the class are planning parties on the same night. You may want to coordinate your plans with other graduates-to-be and throw one big party.

Invitations available at all stationers are ideal for the occasion, since very few of these parties are formal. You may write "R.S.V.P." at the bottom, followed by a telephone number, or you may prefer to write "Regrets only."

There are very few rules about a graduation party. It may be a dance at home or in a club or hall, a dinner party, a barbecue, or a picnic. Your guest list could include friends and family.

You may hold it on graduation night or anytime thereafter, but you should *not* hold the party before you have received word that you are to graduate. Guests at a big celebration should not be expected to bring presents. Whatever type of party you plan, you and your parents should stand near the door and greet the guests. This is not a formal receiving line, but the party is in your honor, and as guest of honor, whatever your age, you should be standing where the arrivals can greet and congratulate you.

If the party is a seated family dinner, and if the graduate is a girl, she sits on her father's right; a boy would sit on his mother's right—the places of honor. As guest of honor you may choose who sits on your other side, and where the other guests sit. If, at a larger party, there are a number of small tables, you should feel free to choose the people you want to sit with you. You may want your parents there, or you may prefer to sit with a group of your closest friends.

ENGAGEMENT AND WEDDING PARTIES

Engagement parties are held to celebrate or announce a newly affianced couple's engagement. Although the guest list can be unlimited, the majority of engagement parties are restricted to relatives and good friends. Engagement gifts are not expected from friends and acquaintances. Gifts, if given at all, are usually given only by relatives and very special friends and generally to the bride alone. Unless the custom in your family or your area is to bring gifts to the engagement party, in which case they are opened as part of the party, they should not be given at that time. It can cause embarrassment to those who have not brought anything.

A wedding party is held to celebrate a wedding that has already occurred either in a private ceremony with few or no guests or one that has taken place some distance away. Wedding parties can range from intimate affairs among close friends and family to elaborate celebrations. A wedding party replaces the reception as the celebratory party for the newly wedded couple. Wedding parties should be held within a reasonable length of time from the actual betrothal and are usually dependent on the couple's schedule. The couple generally acts as host and hostess and provides the food, drinks, and entertain-

Celebration Rituals

ment—and the form of the party is entirely up to them. Guests can bring wedding gifts to the party, although by that time they may have already responded to the news of their friends' wedding with a gift.

FAMILY REUNIONS

Organizing a family reunion may be time consuming, but the results are worth it. You may find yourself having to track down long-lost relatives, particularly if your family hasn't held a reunion before. The trick is to start early; if, for example, you plan a summer reunion, start contacting people at the start of the New Year or even earlier. You should also delegate responsibilities: have one or two people organizing food; another mailing invitations; another preparing any list of participants or a family tree; another arranging accommodations for out-of-town guests. If someone in your family enjoys collecting family memorabilia, have him put it in a scrapbook for display. Someone else could write a brief history of the family or put together a photographic history. Or have a relative compile recipes to create a family cookbook.

The reunion venue can be the old family homestead or a convenient meeting spot for most of the family. The date for the party could be based on a significant event in the family history. Many people rent halls or restaurants; others opt for outdoor picnics, with chairs, umbrellas, and picnic tables covered with pretty tablecloths. If you have volunteers or feel that you won't offend others, you can ask for a small donation to help defray the costs of the rental hall or hire a photographer or videographer to take photographs or movies. Or you can have disposable cameras placed on each table and let relatives take their own pictures; use the kitty to develop the film and send copies to each family.

FAREWELL PARTIES

Farewell, or going-away, parties are an opportunity to gather friends together for one last afternoon or evening with those who are leaving. Because the guests of honor cannot be expected to reciprocate by giving a party and inviting those who have entertained them, they should, more than in other cases, do more than say "Thank you," no matter how busy they may be getting ready to leave. One way to do this is to send flowers or a small gift to the hostess either before or after the party.

If you are planning a party for someone who is leaving town for good, coordinate your efforts with other friends. There is the story of one popular couple who were given something like 13 farewell parties when they moved away from the town in which they'd been living. By the time the departure date arrived, their exhausted friends could hardly wait for them to go! So if you find that your friends are being overly feted, plan something different—take them to the theater, a baseball game, or their favorite restaurant.

HOUSEWARMINGS

If you have just moved or have done extensive decorating on a new home, a housewarming party is in order. You may send invitations on informal notepaper or commercial fill-in cards, or you may simply extend your invitations by telephone. Since the purpose of your party is to welcome friends and open your home to them, expect to spend a good deal of your time giving tours, unless you are comfortable having guests wander through the house without you. Plan accordingly so that someone is always present to answer the front door and welcome guests when you are on tour.

A housewarming is generally a cocktail party or a cocktail buffet. It may be as simple or as elaborate as you wish.

Gifts to celebrate your new home are brought to the party. If the group is small enough and everyone has brought a gift, opening the presents can be a part of the festivities. If the housewarming is more of an open house, however, with guests coming and going, then you should either open gifts as they are presented to you, or set them aside to open after the party, making sure to send a thank-you note as soon as possible thereafter.

RELIGIOUS CEREMONIES
FOR NEWBORNS

Ceremonies honoring a new life are among the most joyous of occasions. Invitations can be given over the telephone or by personal note. The latter makes sense if the guests are from out of town.

THE CHRISTENING PARTY

Although it is not necessary, a reception is often held to celebrate the christening or baptism, where guests eat and drink to the health and prosperity of the baby girl or boy. This reception varies in extravagance among different ethnic groups more than among different religions. When possible, an at-home reception for close family and friends enables the baby to be put to bed for a nap and the parents to relax and enjoy their guests. The reception may be a brunch directly following the ceremony or a gathering for christening cake, generally an elaborately iced white cake, and champagne or punch.

JEWISH CEREMONIES FOR NEWBORNS

Brith Milah. A healthy male child is initiated into the Jewish community on the eighth day after birth through the Brith Milah ("covenant of circumcision") in Hebrew and *bris* ("covenant") in Yiddish. The circumcision is accompanied by a religious ceremony during which the boy is named. The ceremony generally takes place at home, although sometimes it occurs at a synagogue. After the ceremony, there is a joyful meal—often a brunch, as the Brith Milah is usually held early in the day. Relatives and close friends are invited by telephone since the time between birth and the ceremony is short. An invited guest is expected to bring a gift to celebrate the child and the ceremony.

Naming Ceremonies. Girls are named in the synagogue on the first Sabbath that falls closest to 30 days after birth, when the father is called up to the Torah. The naming ceremony is the *brit,* which means "the covenant of the daughter," or the *brit hayyim,* which means "the covenant of life." The mother may be present, as well as the child. In some Reform congregations boys are also named in the synagogue (in addition to being named at the Brith Milah) when both parents are present, and a special blessing is pronounced by the rabbi. Friends and relatives may be invited to attend the religious service and sometimes a reception follows. A small gift for the child is generally given by invited guests.

Redemption of the Firstborn. The ceremony of redemption of the firstborn, the *pidyon haben,* takes place only if the firstborn is a boy, the birth was not Cesarean, and the pregnacy was the first for the mother, including any that ended in miscarriage or stillbirth. It may be performed when the baby is 31 days old (unless that day is the Sabbath or a religious holiday). According to ancient custom described in the Bible, the firstborn son was dedicated to the service of God. It became customary for a *kohen* (a descendant of the priestly tribe) to redeem the child from his obligation, entrusting him to the care of his father for upbringing in the Jewish faith. The *pidyon haben,* consisting of a brief ceremony and a celebration, generally is held in the home. It is practiced by traditional Jews today, but usually not by Reform congregations, which instead focus on the synagogue naming of all the children of a family. Informal notes of invitation to a Redemption ceremony are sent about 10 days beforehand to close friends and relatives.

A Tree for a New Baby. In some Jewish communities, it is traditional to plant a tree to mark the birth of a child. A cedar is chosen for a boy; a pine or cypress tree is chosen for a girl. In the old tradition, the trees, which grew with the children, furnished the wood for the *huppah* poles when they were married.

OTHER RELIGIOUS CELEBRATIONS FOR A NEW BABY

Those who are fortunate to number among their friends people of cultures and religions different from their own should never hesitate to ask their friends about what to do when invited to attend a celebration within the tradition of the other culture or religion. What is important is that friends are able to participate in the welcome to the child.

Hindu Birth Ceremony. This ceremony is held for naming a Hindu baby. It generally occurs when the baby is from six to eight months old, and is referred to as the "rice-eating ceremony," usually marking the first time the child eats solid food. It is most often held at the child's home, and a gift is taken by invited guests. No special clothing is required, but attire should be of the same formality as one would wear to one's own religious services. A reception may be held both before and after the ceremony.

Akikah. Some Muslims practice this Islam birth ceremony. Among those who do, the form the ceremony takes varies greatly but always is a welcome to a newborn infant. A gift is taken by guests to the ceremony, which is generally held in the home of the parents or in a general purpose room in the mosque. Men and women usually sit in different parts of the room. While men generally dress in a shirt and slacks, women should wear a dress or a skirt and blouse. Arms should be covered, and hems should reach below the knees. The head should be covered with a scarf. Neither men nor women guests should wear crosses, Stars of David, or jewelry that depicts signs of the zodiac or the faces or heads of people or animals. A reception may follow.

RETIREMENT PARTIES

Retirements are recognized in a variety of ways, usually by the company or organization from which an individual is retiring. When the recognition is formal it is celebrated at a luncheon or dinner party, with the retiree's immediate family members invited to join people from the department or company. Although these parties may take place in the company dining room or auditorium, they usually are held in the private room of an outside restaurant or a club. Other guests may include those who are involved in the professional life of the retiree.

Sometimes the retirement of a particularly prominent person takes the form of a roast, with speakers called upon to comment on the career of the retiree—generally with a great deal of humor thrown in—and remarks of sincere appreciation and recognition. While retirement parties are usually given by work associates, it is perfectly appropriate for friends or family of the retiree to give a party.

SURPRISE PARTIES

Since surprise parties can take countless forms—in honor of birthdays, new babies, anniversaries, and so on—all that need be said about them is that you must be sure the guest of honor would absolutely enjoy having the surprise, and that you have a fail-safe plan to get him or her to the party. Otherwise, you may be making someone more miserable than happy. If you do decide to go through with the party, the planning and anticipation builds into much excitement for the hosts and guests. The goals are to carry the fun forward for the honoree's sake and to have a memorable party.

CHAPTER 10

LUNCHES, BRUNCHES, AND TEAS

LUNCHES

Lunches can be held in a private home or backyard, a club, a hotel, a restaurant, around a pool—just about anywhere. What often determines the locale are the number of people invited to the lunch and how formal you want it to be. Obviously, the more people, the larger the gathering site.

If your lunch is held at home, the choice of locale is up to you. Set your lunch table in the dining room, on card tables in the living room, or on a patio table for an alfresco meal. The way the table is set depends on the formality of the occasion.

If you are toying with the idea of hosting a lunch in your home, consider how many people you can comfortably accommodate in your dining room or at small individual tables. Consider, as well, the amount of time you can spend on preparation and the help that is available to you.

Invitations may be telephoned or, for more elaborate lunches given in honor of someone, sent on an engraved card. A formal invitation to lunch, however, is more often in the form of a personal note or on a fill-in invitation.

THE LUNCH MENU

Two or three courses are sufficient at any but the most formal lunch, and even then no more than four are served in a private home. Whether you serve cold or hot food is dependent on the season. In summer, light fare, such as a seafood salad and chilled marinated vegetables, make a refreshing meal. In winter, opt for a hot chicken salad and sautéed ratatouille. Mix and match your courses for a well-balanced meal. Hot breads are a welcome feature of every lunch—whether hot croissants, buttermilk biscuits, English muffins, dinner rolls, cornbread, or breadsticks.

A good way to plan your lunch menu is to select from the five possible courses listed below:

1. **FRUIT OR SOUP** If you're not serving fruit for dessert, melon, grapefruit, or a fruit cup is a popular first course. Serve the fruit cup in bowl-shaped glasses that fit into long-stemmed, larger ones with a space for crushed ice between, or in champagne glasses (after being kept cold in the refrigerator) or in individual bowls. Place the fruit cups on small serving plates.

   A clear soup is a smart, light choice for starters. Or, in the winter serve a hearty cream soup; in summer a chilled soup such as vichyssoise or gazpacho hits the spot. Some hosts like to serve a robust soup or stew as the main course. Serve soup with crackers or warm bread.

2. **EGGS OR SHELLFISH** Egg and fish dishes often serve as the lunch's main course. If you offer an egg or shellfish dish, such as a hot seafood casserole, balance that with a light, simple meat dish, such as chicken salad on romaine lettuce, combining the meat and salad courses in one. On the other hand, if you first serve a light pasta, you could follow with meat and vegetables, as well as salad and dessert.

3. **FOWL, MEAT (NOT A ROAST), OR FISH** This course is optional. If you do decide to serve a meat dish, balance it against the egg or shellfish dish you serve before, or combine it with the salad course. Don't discount sandwiches as too informal. Sandwiches can be as fancy as you make them. You can make a delicious lobster salad, for example, and serve it in a croissant. Place the roll on a bed of lettuce and surround it with colorful sliced vegetables. Voilà! You've made an exquisite lobster club sandwich plate.

4. **SALAD** Salad is the mainstay of most lunch menus nowadays. Often, lunch consists merely of soup and a big plate of seafood or Cobb salad, garnished with crudités and breadsticks.

5. **DESSERT** Go for a lighter touch than you would at a dinner party, particularly if a work meeting or a card game is scheduled after lunch. Ice cream and sorbet are always refreshing, especially with a splash of champagne and a dollop of raspberries or blueberries. Fresh fruit is an always welcome palate pleaser; serve with mini lace cookies or chocolates.

LUNCH BEVERAGES

Have a pitcher of iced water or glasses of water already on the table if yours is a seated lunch. Many hostesses like to have coffee or tea served with the meal instead of later. If you offer iced tea, decorate the glasses with sprigs of fresh mint and a lemon slice. Iced coffee should be passed around in a pitcher on a tray that also holds a bowl of sugar, sugar substitute, and a pitcher of milk or cream. From this the guests can pour their own coffee into tall glasses that are half full of ice and accompanied by long-handled spoons. If your lunch is a buffet, make a pitcher of each beverage available close to the buffet table. A bowl of fruit punch may take the place of iced tea or coffee; prepare with floating slices of orange and lemon and surround by glasses or cups adorned with fresh sprigs of mint.

Unless the lunch is a business or club meeting, wine is often served with lunch. One wine is sufficient, and it should be a light one such as sauvignon blanc or a champagne. Wine spritzers (chilled white wine with club soda) are also a nice light choice.

Cocktails may or may not be served before lunch. Lunch cocktails are generally lighter than those offered before dinner. A glass of white wine, a white-wine spritzer, a Bloody Mary, or a mimosa (champagne and orange juice) are typical pre-lunch drinks. As always, offer nonalcoholic drinks along with the cocktails.

THE MEAL

When all the guests have arrived and have had time to enjoy a cocktail or a refreshing drink, the hostess says, "Shall we go in to lunch?" If there is a guest of honor, the hostess leads the way to the dining room, walking beside her or him.

For a formal lunch the hostess may need help in the kitchen or serving. If more than one person is giving the lunch, the duties can be divided among them, eliminating the need for temporary help.

The table setting for a formal lunch is identical to that of dinner. Carving is done in the kitchen, and except for ornamental dishes of fruit, candy, and nuts, no food is set on the table. The plate service is also the same as at a formal dinner. Place settings are never left without plates, except after the salad course

Lunches,
Brunches,
and Teas

when the table is cleared and crumbed for dessert. The dessert plates are arranged as for dinner.

You can also save time by having the first course already on the table and by limiting the main course to a single dish and salad, making it easy to serve. A big seafood salad can be prepared in advance and placed in single bowls or plates. At a less formal lunch, you can have your guests serve themselves family-style from large bowls or platters. If there is no first course, the salad may already be on the table. Rolls, butter, and iced water and any other beverage can also be put on the table beforehand.

Remove any bread-and-butter plates before dessert, along with salt-and-pepper shakers. During dessert, bring out the coffee tray and pour coffee for anyone who wants it.

THE LUNCH BUFFET

If you don't have the help of a server, make your formal party a buffet lunch. The food is set out as for a buffet dinner, on the dining-room table or on any table with sufficient space. The fare, however, should be much simpler and lighter than for a dinner.

Courses offered before the entrée should already be on the table when your guests arrive. Guests should be seated and finish these courses before going to the buffet table for the main course. When there is no serving staff to help, the guests take their empty plates and leave them on a side table as they go to get their next course. Then, while they are helping themselves, you can remove the soiled dishes to the kitchen.

The same procedure is followed when guests are ready for the salad or dessert. When they have finished they can either drink their coffee where they are or leave the tables and sit on comfortable chairs in another room, perhaps. This gives you a chance to clear away glasses, silver, and cloths from the table, and, if bridge is to follow, to set out the cards.

BRUNCHES

This popular form of casual entertaining is a combination of breakfast and lunch but is generally held closer to the usual hour for lunch. Brunch is the perfect entertainment for spur-of-the-moment weekend gatherings—post-wedding celebrations among out-of-town guests, for example, or get-togethers with old friends who are in town for a special event or who are passing through the area on a business trip. No such excuse is necessary, however, if you and your friends simply find the late-morning hours a convenient time to meet.

Informality is the rule, in both dress and demeanor. Because brunch is usually restricted to Saturdays and Sundays only, guests are encouraged to linger at the table for a long, leisurely meal. Invitations may be telephoned ahead of time, but this kind of party is so casual that the host may simply invite his friends as they are leaving another gathering. "Why don't you come over around 11:30 tomorrow morning for brunch?"

Bloody Marys are a popular brunch drink, whether served with or without liquor. Also popular is the mimosa, an icy combination of champagne and chilled orange juice. Don't forget to provide pitchers of fruit juices, pots of coffee or tea, and sodas.

Food can be set out on a buffet table—less elaborately than for lunch or dinner but attractively and conveniently laid out. The menu generally offers a choice of traditional breakfast and lunch dishes, alone or combined. Pair a mushroom omelet, for example, with ratatouille or a tomato salad. Or offer creamed chicken to serve over waffles.

TEA: THE REVIVAL OF A CLASSIC

Long considered the domain of the stodgy and the fuddy-duddy, tea is back in style. Many hotels are offering afternoon teas, complete with delectable tea sandwiches and desserts in comfortable living-room–type settings. You can throw a cozy tea in your own home for just about any reason, whether to honor an out-of-town friend or new neighbor, to "warm" a new house, or to introduce a visiting relative. Invitations to an informal tea are almost always telephoned. However, if the occasion is more formal, you may send a written invitation on either a fill-in card or personal notepaper.

Teatime behavior is relaxed and informal. You can serve from a dining-room table or a tea table set up in any room that has adequate space and easy access. Guests should be able to sit or circulate freely without becoming trapped for the duration in a corner after they have been served.

TEATIME

Set a large tray at both ends of the table, one for tea and one for coffee. One tray is used to bring in all the equipment necessary for the proper serving of tea: a full pot of brewed tea, a pot with boiling water, tea bags if the tea is not made with loose tea, a small pitcher of milk or cream, a sugar bowl, and thin slices of lemon. These days, herbal and decaffeinated teas are popular; include a selection for your guests.

The coffee tray is simpler. The coffee is in a large urn or pot (electric is fine). A pitcher of milk or cream and a bowl of sugar complete the tray. It's a good idea to include sugar substitutes, too. If chocolate is served instead of coffee, there is nothing needed other than the pot of steaming chocolate. Note: Do not light the flames under the pots before the trays are set down; that way you will avoid the danger of fire.

Cups and saucers are placed within easy reach of those who are pouring, usually at the left of the tray, because they are held in the left hand while the tea (or coffee) is poured with the right. If the person pouring is left-handed, she could, of course, reverse the order. On either side of the table are stacks of little tea plates, with small napkins folded on each one. Arranged behind these, or in any way that is pretty and uncluttered, are the plates of food and necessary silver. Forks should be on the table if cake with soft icing is served. If the table is not large enough to hold all the plates, place some on a sideboard or a small table in a convenient location.

A tea bag should never be served in a cup of tea. Preferably, tea is steeped in a pot and then poured into cups and served. Sometimes, however, a host or hostess will indeed bring you a cup with the tea bag floating inside. When this happens, lift the bag from the cup with the spoon when the tea is the strength you like, hold it at the top of the cup while it drains, and place it on the saucer under the cup. Do not wind the string around the spoon and squeeze the tea bag dry. When tea is served in mugs and there is nowhere but the table to put the tea bag—which is unacceptable—ask the hostess where you can put the tea bag.

Many restaurants serve tea by bringing individual pots of hot water to the table for each tea drinker. Each pot is served on a saucer accompanied by one or more tea bags. Place the tea bag into the pot and allow the tea to steep. When the tea reaches the strength you enjoy, remove the bag and place it on the saucer.

TEATIME FOOD

Food for a tea party is quite different from that served at a cocktail party. For one thing, much of the food is sweet—cookies, cupcakes, scones, or slices of cake—and often bite-size. In addition, most teas feature tea sandwiches, generally miniature cold sandwiches made on thin bread. In the winter you might welcome your tea guests with a tray of hot cheese puffs, pastries filled with mushrooms, or a warm artichoke dip. Sandwiches should be light and delicate, such as:

- Watercress and an herb mayonnaise rolled in thin bread
- A cucumber slice on a round of bread with a dollop of salmon roe
- Cream cheese on datenut bread
- Crabmeat salad on pumpernickel bread
- Smoked salmon and cream cheese on round toast

Guests may return to the tea table as many times as they wish but, as at any social function, should not overload their plates at any one time. If you are a tea-party guest, you aren't expected to stay until the very end at a large tea. When you're ready to go, simply thank your host and hostess and bid the guest of honor good-bye.

Because nothing needs to be passed to the guests, it is easy for anyone to give a formal tea without serving help. It's a good idea to appoint a close friend or two to help with the pouring, however. Have him or her give guests a choice between strong and weak tea and ask whether they prefer sugar, milk, cream, or lemon. If you have no help, simply set out the tray with everything except the boiling water before guests arrive, leaving the kettle on the stove in the kitchen. Greet your guests at the door, tell them where to leave their coats, and when you are ready for tea, simply fill the teapot from the kitchen kettle and carry it to the tea table.

BREWING THE PERFECT CUP OF TEA

There is no magic involved in making a first-rate cup of tea. The most important part of the tea service? Boiling water, and plenty of it. To start, first fill a pot halfway with boiling water, let it stand a moment or two to heat the teapot, and then pour it out. Put in a rounded teaspoonful of tea leaves or one tea bag for each cup. Half this amount may be used if the tea is of superb quality. Then pour on enough actually boiling water to cover the tea leaves about half an inch. Tea should steep at least five minutes (or for those who like it very strong, 10) before additional boiling water is poured on. When serving, pour half tea, half boiling water for those who like it weak. Increase the amount of tea for those who like it strong. The cup of good tea should be too strong without the addition of a little lively boiling water, which gives it freshness.

When tea has to stand a long time for many guests, the ideal way to keep it hot and tasting fresh is to make a strong infusion in a big kettle on the kitchen stove. Return the tea to the stove, letting the tea actually boil three to four minutes on the range; then pour it through a sieve or filter into your hot teapot. The tea will not become bitter, and it does not matter if it gets quite cold. The boiling water poured over no more than a tablespoon of such tea will make the drink hot enough.

CHAPTER 11

BARBECUES AND PICNICS

THE BARBECUE

The backyard barbecue is one of the most delightful and quintessentially all-American ways to entertain informally. And because it is so informal, a barbecue is one of the easiest parties to put on.

PLANNING A BARBECUE

Since the setting is outside, disposable plates, cups, and utensils are appropriate. There should be tables and chairs for everyone, or at least comfortable places to sit. Picnic tables don't necessarily need tablecloths, but plastic ones can be pretty and practical. You can fashion an easy centerpiece by placing fresh-cut flowers in copper kettles or earthenware jugs.

For an evening barbecue, make sure the chef has enough light to see what he is cooking and the guests to be able to maneuver easily. Floodlights directed into the trees give a beautiful effect, as do colorful Japanese paper lanterns or candles placed in hurricane lamps. Citronella candles are an excellent idea for a summer night, since they help keep insects away.

THE BARBECUE MENU

A barbecue menu features a main dish, whether meat, fish, vegetables, or fowl, prepared on the grill. Some people prefer to serve dishes that can be eaten as finger food, such as hamburgers or barbecued ribs. If you choose to serve steak, however, be prepared with knives and sturdy plastic plates or china—if you use flimsy paper plates, your guests will have a hard time cutting their steaks without tearing the plate. Other dishes, such as potato salad, coleslaw, or baked beans, can be prepared in advance and kept indoors until you're ready to serve them.

Beer, any soft drink, and wine all go well with the informality of a barbecue. In hot weather, iced tea, iced coffee, and icy sangria are delicious. Keep pots of coffee hot on the grill for serving either during or after the meal.

Cocktails may be served, but since barbecue is generally hearty and rib-sticking, elaborate hors d'oeuvres are not necessary. A few dishes of nuts or potato chips, crudités, and dips scattered about are sufficient.

If you're serving hamburgers, hot dogs, or steak, load up a side table with a variety of condiments, like ketchup, mustard, relish, and steak sauce.

THE PICNIC

Picnics can be utterly delightful when well managed, but they can flop when poorly executed. The idea behind picnics is that much of the food is prepared at home and then moved to an outdoor setting, generally a pretty park, a beach, or a designated picnic site, where it is served. The trick is making sure your moveable feast has a smooth transition. Here are a few general directions for avid picnickers.

PLANNING A PICNIC

You can organize a picnic on your own, inviting guests by telephone. Or you can arrange a group picnic, where you offer to bring the main dish and have each guest contribute a dish, condiments, drinks, or paper goods. Lastly, a group of friends may simply arrange to picnic together, each person or family bringing their own food and cooking it over a community fire. This sort of picnic is especially fine when children are included, as parents know best what their young ones will eat most happily.

If you are hosting a picnic on your own, your first task is to consider your guest list carefully. Nothing is so dampening to the enjoyment of a picnic as the presence of one or more faultfinders who never lift a finger but sit and complain about the heat, the wind, a possible shower, the discomfort of sitting on the ground, or their personal sufferings caused by bugs and flies. If, on the other hand, you select your company from friends who really enjoy picnics, not only will they make everyone forget blowing sand and inquisitive ants, but most likely they will work like beavers.

You then should plan as carefully as you would if you were inviting people to dine with you at home. Make sure that you serve the food without too much delay—preferably within an hour of your guests' arrival (unless you have planned a specific activity beforehand). Consider as well the ages and preferences of your guests when planning your picnic. If your guest list includes several elderly or infirm individuals, make sure there are plenty of folding chairs. Ask guests to bring extra blankets.

THE PICNIC MENU

You can choose to prepare all of your picnic food beforehand—taking only things that are ready to serve, like sandwiches, cold chicken, or a pasta salad— or you can bring a few prepared foods and cook the rest on a grill.

The best kinds of picnics are the simplest, with the one main requirement being that the food be fresh and of good quality.

The simplest type of picnic is a continental one—as if straight from the farms of Europe. It consists of a loaf of bread, a piece of cheese, a container of marinated olives, and a bottle of wine. If the cheese and wine are good and the bread fresh, this menu has all the advantages of being delicious and nourishing, requiring no preparation, and being moderate in cost. However, in spite of the ease of getting together and carrying the ingredients of a continental picnic, most Americans prefer to expand the menu in varying degrees. Using the items above as a base, you may add whatever you wish—fresh tomato, basil, and mozzarella sandwiches, for example, or an olive and sun-dried–tomato pasta.

Some picnics can be feasts of seasonal fresh foods. Cold boiled lobster or steamed shrimp accompanied by coleslaw, a fresh corn salad, and fresh summer berries make a meal that is truly fit for a king. Grilled meat or fish, whole potatoes or corn wrapped in foil and roasted in the coals, and a mixed green salad make a perfect meal. Top it off with cold sliced watermelon or hand-cranked homemade ice cream.

Plates for a picnic that includes hot foods should be more substantial than uncoated paper. You can use plastic or enameled ones, even though they must be taken home to be washed. Plastic bowls or cups for chowder are more leakproof and easier to hold than paper cups. As long as you are bringing the utensils for this type of meal, there is no reason not to accompany your main dish with a salad already mixed in a big bowl and breads kept warm by several layers of foil wrapping. Don't forget to pack coffee or tea in a thermos and carry a cooler full of beer and soft drinks. Stock up on freezer packs to keep foods really cool on hot summer days. This also helps prevent food spoilage, a hazard in warm weather when food is not kept cold enough.

LEAVING THE PICNIC SITE

No matter where your picnic has taken place, be sure not only to tidy up before you leave, but to be careful not to throw trash carelessly aside during the festivities. Many of our highways have pleasant wayside parks for picnickers, equipped with rustic tables, safe drinking water, and waste receptacles. Whether you're on public or private property, you'll need to follow a most important rule of backpackers: Carry out everything you bring in.

Most important of all, *never* leave a fire without being absolutely certain that it is out. In the woods water may be poured on the logs until there is no sign of steam; or if you have a shovel or other means of lifting them, embers may be put out and then buried. On the beach a fire should also be put out with water. *Never* cover the coals with sand until they are completely cool, as they will retain the heat for hours, and someone walking by with bare feet, unable to see the remains of the fire, may step on the hot sand and suffer a terrible burn.

TAILGATE PICNICS

The origin of the tailgate picnic lies in the station wagons of old, the ones with the big, heavy tailgates that were lowered and used as a table for food and fixings, generally in the parking lot outside a football stadium or other sports site. These days it is not necessary to have a tailgate to have a tailgate party. Some people use the back of a sports utility vehicle; others simple bring along a folding table. The only other piece of equipment you may need is a grill. You don't even need a football game to enjoy a delightful picnic with friends; how about a tailgate party before a concert, for example, or during a day at the races?

Tailgate picnics are particularly suitable on two occasions. First, if you are making a long trip and don't want to take too long a break for lunch, you can simply pull over to the side of the road. A roadside rest area is a good place to let down the "tailgate," spread your picnic out, and eat. The second occasion is

an extremely popular tailgating event: the festive lunch before a college or professional football or baseball game. Many friends often turn up in the same parking lot, some with portable grills for cooking T-bone steaks and foil-wrapped potatoes. Some tailgate party enthusiasts even have elaborate five-course lunches already prepared, topped off by wine.

CHAPTER 12

HOUSEGUESTS

The best possible advice one can give to hosts and hostesses who are planning to entertain guests for several days and nights is simply this: communicate clearly.

Make your initial invitation clear. State the dates and times the invitation covers, and include your plans so that they'll know how to prepare. If you are having a formal dinner party during your houseguests' visit, let them know ahead of time so that they bring appropriate clothing. The same is true if you are planning a golf or boating trip, or a swimming day at the beach. If you are inviting city friends for a weekend of sailing or camping, however, let them know that you will provide the equipment; your guests should not be expected to buy expensive gadgets for one weekend's use.

Communicate *during* the visit, as well. Show guests not only where their room, bathroom, towels, and other items are, but also where the refrigerator is. They should be made to feel comfortable helping themselves to snacks or beverages. If something is off-limits, say so. "Please don't wait for me to offer. Help yourself to anything you see except the strawberries—they're for dessert tomorrow night."

Share your plans. If Saturday is your morning to sleep in a little bit, tell your guests so, and show them where the English muffins are or how to start the coffeemaker. If you have to go to a meeting Monday morning, leave the car keys if you have an extra car and tell your guests when you will return.

When good friends are visiting, don't be afraid to ask them to help, and don't, in your anxiety to be sure guests relax and have a good time, refuse their offers. Most guests sincerely want to help and feel uncomfortable if constantly rebuffed or if left to sit while you do all the work.

It's of primary importance for the houseguests to tell the hosts precisely when they are arriving *and* when they are leaving. If your host is expecting you to stay through Sunday evening, stay through Sunday evening. Don't plan at the last minute to leave after breakfast, because your host most likely has planned two more meals or may have refused another invitation to be with you. The following are some words of advice for houseguests.

- Never ask if you may bring a pet along on a visit. Animal lovers they may be, but your weekend hosts probably do not want a strange dog on the premises—one who may or may not get along with their own dog and whose manners may be found wanting. Your request puts the host in a difficult position. If, however, you simply cannot travel without your pet, thank your host and explain that you'll have to refuse as you don't travel without your pet. If your hostess then suggests that you bring it along, you may.

- If your pet is invited, you need to make sure that it behaves. If, on your weekend visit to someone else's home, you introduce a pet who is not housetrained, who chews things, or who freely lounges on furniture or laps, you risk damaging your relationship with your hosts. Do make sure to clean up after your pet and offer to repair or replace any broken or chewed items.

- It is not only courteous but obligatory to give your host or hostess a gift—and, if they have children, to take presents to them. Give your gift to your hostess as soon as you arrive. If you send it later, be sure to do it as soon as possible. Another option: Find the perfect hostess gift while you are visiting.

- Just as it is incumbent upon you to share your arrival and departure plans with your hostess, so is it important to let her know if you have other plans. If, for example, she lives in the same town as another friend with whom you would like to visit, say so in advance. Determine the best day and time for you to make your visit, and make sure

it doesn't disrupt your host's schedule. If you don't communicate this ahead of time and simply announce that you are leaving for a few hours in the middle of your visit, you may be spoiling an activity organized for your pleasure. Knowing ahead that you will be occupied for a period of time gives her the opportunity to do some personal errands.

If you run into other friends in the area and they invite you and your hosts over for a swim or to play tennis, you should never accept the invitation without checking with your hostess beforehand.

- If you plan to take your host and hostess out to dinner one evening during a stay of three days or more, discuss this ahead of time rather than surprising them at the last minute. Again, letting them know ahead of time enables them to plan appropriately for your visit. Otherwise your hostess may already have planned and prepared a special meal at home.
- If your hostess is a good friend, offer to bring food for an evening's meal. Your hostess will probably be happy to accept such an offer. On an informal weekend, guests feel more comfortable if they can contribute—and it certainly pleases the hostess.
- Both weekend guest and hostess need time apart from each other. Let your hostess know that you jog an hour every day unless there is something you can do with her instead. This gives her the opportunity to say, "Good for you! While you're out I'll get to tackle some work I need to do for a Monday meeting."
- Be adaptable. You must always be ready for anything—or nothing. If the plan is to picnic—and you can't bear picnics—graciously and enthusiastically soldier through the experience.
- Remember that wise adage, "Neither a borrower nor a lender be." Try to take everything you need with you. But if you *must* borrow, return the article as soon as you can and in good shape. If you borrow a book from your hosts, don't dog-ear it by turning the corners of the pages down; find a piece of paper to use as a bookmark. Don't go home with a book you have started without your host's permission. If he does suggest that you take it home, return it promptly unless he tells you explicitly that he does not want it back.

A Helping Hand

You should never expect your host to wait on you hand and foot. Help out around the house by making your own bed, picking up around your room, and offering to help prepare the meals, clear the table, and clean up in the kitchen.

Be sure to maintain an immaculate bathroom, especially if you are sharing it with other people. Don't leave a ring in the tub, a rim of dried shaving soap in the basin, hair anyplace, or dirt on the soap. A wise hostess leaves a sponge on the basin to help her guests leave a clean bathroom, but if she doesn't, either ask for one or use a paper towel or toilet tissue—never your washcloth—to wipe up after yourself. When sharing a bathroom, don't leave your cosmetics or shaving gear spread all over the available space.

And don't use more than your share of hot water if others are planning to bathe, or dirty up any towels but your own. Finally, leave the toilet seat and the lid down.

On the morning of the day you are leaving, remove the sheets, fold them, place them at the foot of the bed, and pull the blanket and spread up neatly so

TELEPHONE CALLS MADE BY HOUSEGUESTS

Many visitors forget to offer to pay for their calls. The definite rule is this: Should a houseguest be obliged to make a local call or two, he or she would not ordinarily offer payment for it, but it is absolutely required that every long-distance call be paid for. Moreover, this is the only way in which a houseguest can feel free to telephone as often as he or she may want to. The best solution: If you're a guest in someone's home, take along a calling card or telephone credit card or access the operator and arrange to have calls billed to your home number. Another way the guest can pay is to call the operator as soon as the call is finished and ask, for example, for "the toll charge on 212–555–9121." The necessary amount should be left with a slip, giving the date and the number called. If it is a substantial amount, tax should be added. Or if a visitor has used the telephone a great deal during a long stay, the complete list of calls with the amounts of each and their total should be handed to the host or hostess and paid for when the houseguest leaves. No matter how wealthy the host may be, this debt should be paid.

One additional note: Houseguests should not answer the phone while visiting unless they ask, "Would you like me to answer?" or the hostess says "My hands are all wet—would you take that call?" And, when a houseguest answers the phone, he should ask who is calling and offer to take a message.

WHEN THE HOUSEGUESTS ARE FAMILY

As a good hostess, you want all your houseguests to feel that while they are guests in your house they are part of the family. Sometimes, however, when actual family members visit, they forget that they are guests. It's not uncommon to find brothers, cousins, in-laws, nieces, and nephews sprawled all over the house and never lifting a finger to help. A sister may break house rules by eating on the living-room sofa, for example, or a mother-in-law may expect to be waited on hand and foot. In either case, you'll need to gently lay down the law: You might remind your sister of the house rules in a humorous way, say, and ask your mother-in-law if she minds helping you out with a few chores.

Then there are the visits from family members who take over and disrupt the routine of the household. They meddle, advise, and contradict the wishes of the heads of the household. It's unlikely that he or she will have a lasting effect on the household routine—however, if you find yourself resenting this person's visits more and more, it is perfectly OK to explain, in a gentle and nonaccusatory way, that while you know her intentions are good, sometimes her actions make you feel uncomfortable or resentful.

that the bed will look made. If you make it up with your sheets in place, it is all too easy for a busy hostess to forget, and then turn down the beds for the next guest, only to find the dirty sheets still on. Or you may ask your hostess what she would like you to do with the sheets (whether to leave them on or not). If you are close friends and a frequent visitor, go ahead and make the bed up with fresh sheets.

MORNINGS AND BEDTIME

The good houseguest in general conforms to the habits of the family with whom he is staying. He takes his meals at their hours, eats what is put before him, gets up and goes out, and comes in and goes to bed according to the schedule arranged by his hostess. And no matter how much the hours or the food or the arrangements may upset him, he must appear blissfully content.

When the visit is over, he need never enter that house again, but while he is there he must at least act as though he is enjoying himself.

A house-party hostess may properly go to bed before her guests. She should urge her guests to help themselves to a drink or a snack and stay up as long as they want.

If you are particularly good friends and you know you keep different hours than your hosts, you may say that you would like to get up early and tour the town during quiet hours, or whatever, assuring your hosts that you don't want them to get up with you. As to hunger, again with close friends, simply ask if it is all right if you have juice or make toast when you awake, especially when you are visiting with children. Children's tummies can't wait for hosts to get up and fix breakfast. If requesting this makes you uncomfortable or you are visiting people who are not close friends, travel with portable snacks, like granola bars and bottled juices, so that your children's hunger pangs—or yours—can be staved while you wait for breakfast time.

WHEN IT'S TIME TO GO

The most popular and sought-after guests *never* stay longer than planned. The length of the visit should be clearly stated by the hostess and interpreted literally by her guests. If from past experience a hostess knows that certain guests are apt to try to extend their visit, she should make plans for the days after they are to leave so that she can tell them that she'd love them to stay longer, but. . . .

In short, for both guest and hostess, it is far better to end a visit while everyone is still enjoying it.

Overnight visits require written thank-you notes within a day or two of your return home. The only exceptions are when your hosts are relatives or close friends with whom you visit back and forth frequently or whose vacation home you visit often. Even then a call the next day to say, "We're still talking about what fun the weekend was!" is appreciated and really should be made.

SAYING "NO"
TO WEEKEND GUESTS

Q. *My husband and I are members of the geriatric set and are in a dilemma over potential houseguests. Our dear friends from 300 miles away have asked if they could come visit us for an extended period of time. The problem is that they have two youngsters, ages three and five, who are undisciplined and quite a handful, as we discovered when they came to visit last year. My wife and I simply cannot handle these kids in close quarters again. How do we say so to our friends without hurting their feelings?*

A. Very nicely and diplomatically express your situation to them in a letter or over the phone. Tell them that at your age, you simply do not have the energy to have the four of them stay in your home. While making it clear that their visit means a great deal to you, ask whether they wouldn't mind either staying for only one or two nights in your home or staying in a motel nearby. You can even offer suggestions on motels and hotels in the area. And, if your finances are sufficient and you don't think it would insult them, you can even offer to pay for half or all of their motel stay.

CHAPTER 13

CHILDREN'S PARTIES

I t's a proven fact that children can be taught from an early age how to be
gracious hosts and hostesses. As Emily Post so wisely put it, "Children can
scarcely be too young to be taught the rudiments of etiquette." Impress upon
them the importance of making guests feel comfortable and welcome in their
home.

From the beginning, let them be active participants in their own social life.
Start by having them help plan a party and create their own invitations.

Talk to both very young and older children about the activities they want
to have at their parties. Help them to learn negotiating skills—when one friend
wants to play badminton and the other wants to watch television, the young
host can say, "Let's play badminton for an hour and then have a snack and
watch TV."

Children who are guests need help, too. Younger children need to know
what to say when they are served a food they don't like, as well as what to do
when their friend is bossy, overbearing, or boring. Most important, if something
goes wrong when they are visiting another child, they have to know how to
extricate themselves from the situation. For example, you could teach them to
say, "It's getting late, so I think I had better call my mother to come get me."
Older children need to be taught the same skills, as well as all the rules of courtesy, respect for others and their property, and safety when in circumstances
away from home.

When a party is planned, it is incumbent upon parents to be present and
to make their presence known without being in attendance every minute. No
child, not even a teenager, has the skills to deal with peers when a situation gets
out of hand, when "crashers" appear at the door, or in ending a party grace-
fully.

A child who grows up comfortable in managing these skills will undoubtedly become a gracious adult host and guest.

BIRTHDAY PARTIES

Children's birthday parties have certain rituals of their own. Customs vary from community to community. Before launching into an elaborate party for a small child, novices should call a seasoned children's birthday party giver—generally another parent—and ask what is expected.

The younger the child, the shorter, smaller, and simpler the party. Gifts may or may not be part of the proceedings. The very worst custom in some communities is parental competition over children's birthday parties and gifts. If Janie has a pony, Tammy has two ponies. If Sam has a children's Ferris wheel, Andrew rents a mini amusement park. The truth of the matter is that children simply enjoy being together, and the younger they are, the less formal or elaborate or expensive the entertainment they need. Young children, too, may find elaborate events more frightening than enjoyable.

PLANNING THE PARTY

The children's backyard birthday party of old has some serious competition these days, with kids favoring places like the local bowling alley, the skating rink, the pony farm, and fast-food restaurants in which to celebrate birthdays. In addition, children's party spaces have sprung up, big loftlike places catering exclusively to celebrations for children, where the kids can climb over child-proof jungle gyms, jump into vats full of plastic balls, spill food, and play loudly—and the parents can leave the mess for someone else to clean up.

If you are having the party at home, make sure you have more activities planned than you need. Children often race from one game to another, and you may end up having to come up with something more to do on the spot.

PARTY REFRESHMENTS

Parents who monitor their children's intake of sugar may have to either compromise a bit on party day, be there to keep sweets out of their kids' hands, or refuse the invitation altogether. If your child has a physical problem or is allergic to a certain food, explain that to the mother of the birthday child before the party.

At any rate, if you're the host, keep the sweets and the caffeinated soft drinks to a manageable level. Children prefer simple, comforting fare, like hamburgers, hot dogs, pizza, or fried chicken.

Opening the Gifts

If you are a parent with very definite ideas about the sorts of gifts you will allow your young child to have, make that clear in your invitation, whether written or phoned. If you don't allow toy guns in the house, tell your party guests' parents in advance.

Some parents don't let their children open their gifts until everyone has gone home, partly because they want to keep all duplicates intact so they can return or exchange them. There are several compelling reasons, however, to have children open their gifts in front of their friends. First, it is one of the moments of the party where the birthday child is in the limelight. Second, other children are often excited about the gift they are giving and are anxious to see him or her open it and express pleasure. Third, it is an opportunity for children to use their best manners by thanking their friends—and they should be told ahead of time to graciously thank the person who gave a duplicate gift or a peculiar one.

When the gift is opened and the donor is thanked personally at the time of the opening, a thank-you note is not necessary—although writing notes is a habit well worth teaching at an early age. If the gifts are opened later, the birthday child should definitely write a personal note, mentioning the gift by name, to every donor.

Party favors are generally given to guests as they leave the party. A colorful bag of inexpensive toys, crayons, or candy treats, perhaps, is a nice gesture. You can also take a Polaroid of each child with the birthday honoree and give it to each when he or she leaves.

Sleep Overs

Whether your slumber party guests are elementary-school age or teenagers, your house rules must be respected. You have every right to enforce these rules, and your children's guests are expected to honor your wishes. Make sure they clearly understand the house rules on such issues as bedtime, watching television, noise, and cleaning.

When a teenager goes to spend a long weekend with friends, the same basic rules apply as do for adults. The visitor should take a gift, preferably a "house" present rather than a "hostess" present. A game, plant, movie on video—anything that can be enjoyed by the whole family—are good choices.

If your teen is a houseguest-to-be, remind him before going to be polite and helpful—not only to his friend, but to his friend's parents and siblings. Remind him to pick up after himself, to make his bed, and to leave the bathroom clean. He should *not* leave socks, shoes, and sweaters, for example, lying around the house. Even though the menus may not offer his favorite foods, he should try everything and keep his feelings to himself if he is disappointed. He must, of course, obey any household rules laid down by his friend's parents.

Finally, make sure your teenager writes a thank-you letter to his friend's mother. He need not write his friend if they will see one another soon, but the bread-and-butter letter to the mother is a must. This is not at all necessary, but always appreciated, for the casual sleep over at a friend's house on a Friday or Saturday night; a verbal thanks in the morning will suffice.

SKATING AND BOWLING PARTIES

A popular treat for kids is a party in a roller-skating rink, an ice-skating rink, or a bowling alley. If you're the host, you'll need to make certain arrangements in advance. First, get a head count and make sure the rink or alley will be able to accommodate your group. You may need to order food ahead of time, or at least determine what foods are available. If you are hosting a party for kids under 12, make sure you have a sufficient number of adults to supervise the group. Parents hosting a child's skating or bowling party pay for the group's rink or bowling-alley tickets, bowling shoes or skates, and food. (Call ahead to check on special group rates.) They should also make sure that each child has reliable transportation to and from the party site.

CHAPTER 14

BYOB AND BYOF PARTIES

BYO" means "bring your own" bottle or food, whichever the case may be. Such parties serve a real purpose, but they also can cause resentment, so one should be careful in planning this sort of affair. Nonetheless, bring-your-own parties are great for neighborhood gatherings, get-togethers with close friends or office mates, or last-minute celebrations.

BYOB

"Bring-your-own-beverages" parties are usually planned by a group that wants the costs of a social event to be shared or by people who are on a tight budget and can't possibly entertain a group of friends if they have to provide *all* the refreshments. In the latter case, friends are called upon to provide the liquid refreshment while the host or hostess provides the food, mixers, and soft drinks. In a written invitation, all that is necessary is a "BYOB" in the corner of the invitation.

The bottles brought to these parties are *not* intended to be gifts for the host and hostess. They simply make it possible for the group to get together without anyone's incurring an enormous expense. It is fine, therefore, for each attendee to take just the amount of beverage he or she plans to drink at the party. The bottles should be sealed, however, as it is illegal in many states to transport open liquor bottles in cars. For this reason, any opened bottles should remain at the host's house at the end of the party. Bottles usually are pooled during the party, and if one couple runs out of Scotch, for example, they are offered some by one of the other Scotch drinkers.

BYOF

"Bring-your-own-food," or potluck, parties are given for much the same reasons as BYOB parties. The hosts want to bring friends together and have a good time, but they can't afford to do it all, so everyone is asked to chip in. This is perfectly all right, but it comes with a big "if." That is, *if* it is made clear *when the invitation is extended* that it is a potluck party. Misunderstandings and resentments occur when a guest accepts an invitation and is *then* told that he or she is expected to bring a casserole or perhaps contribute money.

A hostess who arranges this sort of evening is not technically giving the party—she is organizing it. There are several ways of doing it. She may call several people and say, "Let's get a group together. We'll all bring one dish, and I'll have a keg of beer on hand." Or she may do it on her own by sending written invitations asking each person to provide a specific dish. In this case she would write "Come to a Potluck Dinner" at the top. Unless she has specified a dish *and* a bottle, she should provide the liquid refreshments. The important thing is that she make it quite clear that she is not giving the entire party—*before* the guest accepts. The invitees are then free to refuse the invitation if they are unwilling or unable to contribute.

In spite of the obvious advantages of this type of entertaining, it does not take the place of the party you truly give for your friends. As long as you can afford to provide even the simplest food and drink, you should accept the entire responsibility. The host or hostess at a private party should *never* ask for contributions of money to help defray expenses. The only time this is permissible is when the group—official or unofficial—gives a party to celebrate a special event or to raise funds for a cause, and either sells tickets or asks for donations. Again the amount requested must be clearly stated on the invitation, and guests should never be asked to contribute—without warning—at the party.

CHAPTER 15

THEME PARTIES

CARD PARTIES

When giving a card party, whether of two tables or of 10, the first thing to do is to plan the pairings carefully. The tables may all be different—one with good players, another with beginners, one where the stakes are high, another where they play for nothing—but do your best to put those who play approximately the same kind of game at the same table. In addition to skill it's important to remember temperament. Don't put people who take their game very seriously—playing "for blood"—with those who chatter unceasingly and keep asking whose turn it is or whose bid it is. One poor player can spoil the whole party for those who play well.

When a group of friends play together regularly, however, and have more or less the same degree of skill, they may prefer to draw for partners and tables in order to have the opportunity of playing with different combinations of people. They may also move around—changing tables and partners after four hands, two rubbers, or whatever they decide upon. Each player keeps his own individual score. The game is just as much fun but far less cutthroat than conventional play tends to be.

PLANNING A CARD PARTY

Prepare by placing a fresh pack of cards on each table and freshly sharpened pencils beside score pads. On each table leave a slip of paper with the names of the players who are to sit there, or simply tell each guest where he is to play. Make sure that each table is comfortably lighted. Poorly placed light that is reflected from the shiny surface of the cards is just as bad as darkness—and can make hearts and diamonds indistinguishable from spades and clubs. If you have any doubt about the light, sit in each place, hold the cards in your hands, lay a few on the table, and see for yourself.

CARD-PARTY REFRESHMENTS

The kinds of refreshments you offer your card-playing guests depend, of course, on the time of day. On a hot summer day when people have been playing cards for an hour or more, a tray of cold drinks is a welcome sight. Or, keep a pitcher of something cold on a sideboard or buffet table so that guests may help themselves.

While tea sandwiches and petit fours accompanied by tea or coffee are suitable for a 4:00 P.M. game, they don't satisfy at an evening gathering. If dinner is not the evening's agenda, and the card party is running late, at around 10:00 P.M. or 11:00 P.M. put out a selection of cold cuts, cheeses, and a variety of breads for do-it-yourself sandwiches, with coffee and beer, on a dining-room table. Having served themselves, guests can either return to the cleared card tables or take their plates to more comfortable chairs in the living room.

A dessert card party is a happy compromise for the hostess who feels that she cannot provide a full luncheon or dinner for her guests. When the guests are small in number and the hostess has a dining-room table large enough to seat them, dessert may be served on the dining table, set for a dessert course only. Individual place mats are set with a dessert plate, a lunch napkin, a fork at the left, a spoon at the right, and a glass of water. When the guests are seated, the hostess passes the dessert; while they are finishing, she pours coffee, and it is handed around the table. After coffee they begin playing on tables already set up in the living room.

If there are more guests than dining-room chairs, the table may be set as a buffet, using a tablecloth, place mats, round paper or lace doilies under the stack of plates and the dishes on which the dessert is served.

The guests serve themselves and take their plates to the living room. Some hostesses give their guests the option of taking their dessert and beverage to the card tables, where they can eat while they play.

If it is customary in your community to play for prizes, then you must select a first prize for the highest score made by a woman and a first prize for the highest score made by a man. Sometimes a second prize is given. All prizes should be wrapped before being presented. Those who receive prizes must, of course, open the packages at once and show some evidence of appreciation when thanking the hostess.

BOOK OR READING GROUPS

Among the most popular entertainments these days are book clubs, where friends or acquaintances who love to read form a group that meets once a month for discussion. Often the meetings include food and drinks. The convenience of the members determines the hour, and the meeting place is usually rotated among the members.

Refreshments are generally served after the activity of the meeting. The host or hostess may want to provide snacks or cookies and coffee during the book discussion.

Otherwise there are no rules for such groups—except to be firm with those who don't try to keep in tune or with the gossipers who wander from the topic under discussion.

GOURMET COOKING CLUBS

An equally popular entertainment is the formation of gourmet or cooking clubs, where the members of the group—generally from six to 12 people—cook meals for one another. Often, a theme is selected, such as a Mexican or Thai cuisine or favorite comfort foods, and everyone in the club makes a dish that reflects that theme. The venue is held at a different member's home each time the group meets, and the host generally is responsible for sodas, coffee, tea, mixers, condiments, and the table setting. Wine tastings are often a big part of the meal. A gourmet club party is different from other types of entertaining in that it is a good place to boldly try out new recipes.

Gourmet cooking is so in vogue these days that many people enjoy cooking as entertainment. Often the warmest, most relaxed parties are those where you and other guests relax and sip wine at the kitchen table while your host prepares your meal right in front of your eyes—and often regales guests with entertaining stories while he's at it.

TV PARTIES

The television is such an integral part of modern life that parties are often planned around a favorite program or an annual televised event. Academy Award parties, for example, are an excuse for guests to wear campy evening wear and elaborate makeup. Super Bowl and Olympics parties are extremely popular, and are often accompanied by a cold beer and a big stew pot of something hearty. College students favor prime-time soap-opera parties. The rules of TV parties are determined by the host or hostess, with basic thoughtfulness and concern for guests' comfort being the primary requisite. Of course, it is only proper that the host relinquish control of the television remote for the evening to his guests. Either that, or he should consult with friends and family on their preferences before he switches channels.

HALLOWEEN COSTUME PARTIES

Halloween is one of the most popular party nights in the year and allows for much creativity by all. The nice thing about Halloween is that a costume party for kids has many of the same elements as one for adults, and as such can include both. Costumes are de rigueur, of course, as are carved pumpkins, cobwebs, ghosts, and dim lighting. You may also add harvest decor (Indian corn, colorful gourds), typical Halloween games (bobbing for apples), scary recorded music (witch cackles, ghost moans, and the like), and treats like candied apples. The only differences are that adult parties may include alcohol and racier costumes than at kids' parties. Small children should never be left alone at a Halloween party, however, and may prefer face paint to a stuffy mask.

PARTIES WITH A TWIST

Half the fun of a party, for many people, is in the planning. Some people just have a knack for creative party giving. If you're tired of the same old "Cocktails at 6:00," here are a few ideas for something new and different.

MURDER MYSTERY

Many party planners specialize in complete murder-mystery dinners, where guests try to solve a murder mystery much as the weekend houseguests in Agatha Christie's mysteries would do. A less expensive way to go is to buy a murder-mystery party kit, available in game or toy stores.

COME AS YOU ARE

This is a theme that can be greatly expanded upon: Try a Come-As-You-Wish-You-Were party, a Come-As-Your-Favorite-Hero party, a Come-As-Your-Favorite-Villain party, a Come-As-Your-Favorite-Movie-Star party, and on and on.

TIME WARP

This is when everyone comes dressed in the style of a designated decade, the music of that decade is played, and the food of that decade is served. These are especially fun when celebrating a big birthday for someone who was born or came of age in a particular decade.

MAD HATTER

Everyone invited to this party wears a goofy or unique and original hat.

PARTY GAMES AND ENTERTAINMENT

Often, a host or hostess has planned games or entertainment for the evening. It may simply be music, a mystery game, charades, or board games. It is incumbent upon guests to accede to the host's wishes to participate—however ridiculous they may consider the entertainment.

If the entertainment consists of background music during cocktails and dinner, the host should ensure that it is unobtrusive. That means it should generally be instrumental rather than vocal and at a relaxed tempo. It should be at background level, not loud, so that it doesn't interfere with quiet conversation. Good choices: piano arrangements and classical recordings performed by ensemble groups.

CHAPTER 16

LAST-MINUTE ENTERTAINING

A long-lost friend suddenly comes to town; the promotion came through; an important deal is closed. In this busy, hectic world, last-minute gatherings may be the number-one way America celebrates—and can result in some of the most memorable occasions of a lifetime. Get off the couch, break out the bubbly, and celebrate!

TAKE-OUT ENTERTAINING

What would Emily Post think of entertaining with take-out food? She would probably approve and consider it a perfectly fine way to enjoy the company of friends in a casual setting. Today, more and more people have less and less time to prepare elaborate meals. The important issue is that friends have an opportunity to visit with one another.

Take-out entertaining can take many forms. Ordering pizzas or Chinese dishes for a group is one version. Another is blending takeout with a potluck meal, with the host making a big main dish, such as spaghetti or chili, and each guest bringing a take-out dish from a different source to make a complete meal. One guest may bring the bread from a bakery, for example, another guest would bring pastries, and another guest would bring a salad.

Takeout these days doesn't have to be relegated to pizza or hamburgers. Gourmet food stores offer delicious and elaborate dishes to go. Delis will make huge sliced-meat and salad platters. Even mail-order takeout is taking off: Order out and a day later you'll have fresh Florida stone crabs, Vermont hickory-smoked bacon, or Scottish salmon delivered to your door.

Any way you cut it, take-out entertaining is generally a casual affair. So don't fret over correct table settings; in fact, sturdy paper plates, festive paper napkins, and plastic utensils are the tools of choice. As the host or hostess, however, you always want to make your guests feel taken care of and comfortable. That means you should greet your guests enthusiastically, let them serve themselves first, enjoy their company, and give them a warm send-off.

TIPS FOR QUICK MEALS

The 1950s saw the appearance of convenience foods—prepackaged, preprocessed, easy-to-prepare frozen, dry, and canned meals. Indeed, convenience foods revolutionized the cooking industry, freeing housewives from the kitchen. These days, the busy cook doesn't have to rely on preprocessed convenience foods—which are often high in salt, fat, and nonnutritious filler—to prepare quick, delicious meals. The advantage: modern tools and cooking methods that make preparing fresh, nutritious foods a snap. The following are a few tips on preparing complete meals in no time.

- Use your microwave. These timesaving appliances let you (among other things) bake potatoes in no time, quickly heat up leftovers, wilt spinach for spinach salad, cook bacon fast (and with less fat), rapidly thaw frozen foods, and toast nuts.
- Invest in a food processor and a blender.
- Grill whenever you can.
- Freeze pie crusts and puff pastries for quick quiches and pies.
- Don't throw out day-old rice or pasta. For example, you can sauté leftover linguini with olive oil, garlic, sun-dried tomatoes, and olives for a filling meal.
- Keep cold cuts and sliced cheeses on hand for quickie "make-your-own" sandwiches. Your sandwich spread could include jars of grilled marinated peppers, sun-dried tomatoes, and oil-cured olives, all of which have a long shelf life. Always refrigerate after opening, however.
- Always have eggs in your fridge. One of the easiest and most elegant dishes you can whip up is an omelet. Fill with whatever leftover meats and vegetables you have on hand.
- Keep canned meat broths and bouillon cubes on hand; many recipes call for the addition of stocks and broths, and cooking them takes time.
- Stock up on fresh items when they are in season and freeze the overage. If you find a good deal on fresh shrimp in August, for example, buy in bulk and freeze in one-pound containers what you don't use.

FREEZE-AHEAD DISHES

Whenever you're faced with a surplus of food—a neighbor with a garden drops off 10 pounds of tomatoes, for example—it's a smart idea to make a big pot of something, whether tomato sauce, vegetable soup, or chili con carne. Even smarter: Make more than you need and freeze the surplus. That way, anytime you have a last-minute guest or your special dinner flopped, simply thaw the frozen food for a quick home-cooked treat. Casseroles, pasta dishes, soups, and stews will keep in the freezer from six to twelve months. Keep in mind that flavors become somewhat diminished in the freezing process, so you may need to reseason your frozen food a bit when you thaw it.

Consider, as well, stocking up on raw meat, poultry, fish, and fresh vegetables, particularly if you can buy in bulk. When doing so, know the amount of time these foods will keep in your freezer. Most poultry will keep six to seven months; steaks and roasts, six to twelve months; pork chops, three to six months; lean fish, six months; oily fish, three months. Eat fresh-tasting vegetables all winter long. Blanched asparagus or green beans last eight to twelve months; fresh corn cooked and cut off the cob will last twelve months.

Anytime you can, freeze leftover meat and vegetable stocks. One smart way to do this is to set aside an ice-cube tray, pour cooled stock into the tray, and freeze. When you need some chicken stock, for example, simply pop out a cube or two to drop into a dish for richer flavor.

Wrap casseroles and meats in heavy aluminum foil or plastic wrap and then aluminum foil. Put vegetables in freezer bags and squeeze out all the air before sealing. Be sure to label each package and include the date.

THE WELL-STOCKED PANTRY

Stock your kitchen pantry with nonperishable foods in the event of a last-minute celebration. Be on the lookout for sales at your local grocery so that you can buy in bulk. Here are some foods to have around that you can arrange in minutes to serve as appetizers. Don't forget to have a supply of beverages and napkins on hand.

- Jars of salsa
- Jars or cans of nuts
- Tins of minced clams, pâté, and smoked oysters
- Dried soup mixes (combine with sour cream to make great dips)
- Bean dip
- Olive oil and red wine vinegar
- Jars of marinated artichokes
- Jars of sun-dried tomatoes
- Chips, crackers, and microwave popcorn
- Jams and jellies
- Anchovies and anchovy paste
- Jars of marinated sweet peppers

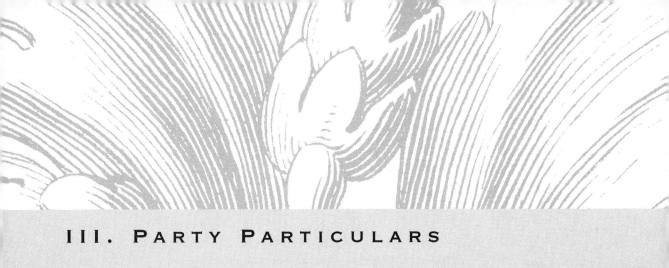

III. Party Particulars

"[To be a good host] don't pretend to be other than you are. In other words, don't dress the chore-man as butler, or the grocery boy as a footman in the hope of impressing your neighbors. To make too much effort is always a mistake. On the other hand, don't lazily and incompetently think that no provision at all is 'plenty good enough.'"

—EMILY POST, *Etiquette* (1922)

CHAPTER 17

THE GOOD HOST

It takes work to entertain successfully. If you do your work in advance, however, with thorough planning and preparation, a dinner or weekend party will be a labor of love not only for your guests, but for you as well. There is nothing more uncomfortable than for guests to feel that their host and hostess are running themselves ragged entertaining them—or that their mere presence is an intrusion on the host household. If you want your guests to be relaxed, you must relax, too.

THE GOOD HOST'S PARTY GUIDE

There is nothing mysterious about hosting well. It involves little more than common courtesy, a nurturing ambiance, and sincere interest in making guests feel comfortable and welcome.

- **BE RELIABLE** Be ready at the hour of the invitation. Don't count on late arrivals and rush to the door with your hair half dried or a dust rag in your hands when guests arrive at the hour at which you've invited them.
- **BE AVAILABLE** Be there to greet guests as they arrive, even if you have to excuse yourself from a conversation with another guest. It is not necessary for both the host and hostess to greet guests at the door.
- **BE PREPARED** Have the table set in advance, and plan meals that do not require you to spend the entire cocktail hour in the kitchen.
- **BE PRECISE** Be clear in your invitation as to the formality of the occasion. Don't write "casual" and open the door wearing satin and diamonds.
- **BE A CATALYST** Make a point of circulating among your guests and introducing strangers to one another, staying with them long enough to get a conversation launched.
- **BE AWARE** Keep an eye on guests' drinks, offering a refill so that they don't have to ask.

- **BE A LEADER** Remember that guests look to you to raise your fork first during dinner; do so promptly so that they may begin eating. Or be sure to say, after the first three or so guests are served, "Please begin eating," so that the food doesn't cool while they wait for you to be served or to serve yourself.
- **BE MINDFUL** Pay attention to details, such as a well-stocked bathroom. A hostess should have guest towels hanging in plain view. Because people often consider linen hand towels to be decorative only, have terry hand towels available. Or place a small stack of nice paper towels beside the sink, to throw away into a wastebasket afterward. Have plenty of extra toilet paper on hand, and a fresh bar of soap in the soap dish.

CHAPTER 18

THE GOOD GUEST

A good guest is enthusiastic, congenial, and considerate, treating other guests and the host and hostess, as well as their property, with thoughtfulness and respect. The most well-mannered guest at any occasion follows the Good Guest's Party Guide, below.

THE GOOD GUEST'S PARTY GUIDE

- **KNOW WHEN TO ARRIVE.** If the invitation is a casual "come at 6:30 or 7:00," split the difference and ring the bell at 6:45, but never later than 7:00. On the other hand, if you have ever arrived at 6:15 to find your hostess just out of the shower, you know it is safe to say that one should never arrive early. When a specific time is given, arrive at the time stated, or shortly thereafter.

- **TAKE SPECIAL CARE NOT TO DAMAGE YOUR HOST'S PROPERTY.** If it is muddy or wet outside, wipe your feet on the doormat. Don't put your feet up on the couch or the coffee table.

- **PUT YOUR DRINK GLASS ON A COASTER** or ask for one if none is in sight.

- **DO NOT SNOOP.** It is rude to tour through someone's house uninvited. Ask your host if he will show you the house.

- **DON'T IGNORE YOUR HOSTESS WHEN SHE ANNOUNCES THAT DINNER IS SERVED.** On the other hand, don't jump up and fly out as if you have been kept waiting to the point of starvation. Watch your hostess, and if she seems to be edging toward the door, take one more sip of your cocktail and rise.

- **PRACTICE BATHROOM ETIQUETTE.** If you use a hand towel, make sure to put it back on the rack, unfolded, so that it is obvious that it has been used. When you wash your hands, wipe off the basin. Before you leave, put the toilet seat and the lid down.

- **DO NOT SMOKE IN ANYONE'S HOME** unless he does so himself. Today, with unanswered questions about the dangers of secondhand smoke, even those who previously didn't mind may mind now. If you must have a cigarette, ask your host or hostess if you can step outside for a few minutes. Never light a pipe or cigar indoors without asking first. Never smoke around infants or small children. When at a party in a club where smoking is allowed, it is still courteous to ask those with you if they mind if you smoke. Lastly, it is bad form to walk around or dance with a cigarette in your hand or hanging from your mouth.

- IF YOU BURN A TABLE OR A RUG, BREAK AN ORNAMENT, OR SNAP THE BACK LEGS OF THE CHAIR, DON'T TRY TO HIDE THE DAMAGE. Apologize at once and arrange to replace the item if possible or to pay for repairs if not. If it is a substantial amount, see if your insurance policy will cover it.

- DON'T USE THE TELEPHONE WITHOUT PERMISSION, and then only if you charge the calls to your credit card or home number. If you have a cell phone, again, it is rude to use it without first asking if your host minds if you make a call. Or, simply excuse yourself to make your calls in the privacy of the guest room.

- DON'T FORWARD PERSONAL CALLS TO YOUR HOST'S HOUSE without asking permission to do so, and then only if you are an on-call professional, are expecting an emergency, or have children who are out and may need to reach you. Then, if you do get calls, keep them brief.

- NEVER VISIT FRIENDS WHEN YOU HAVE A COLD OR OTHER INFECTIOUS ILLNESS. No matter how bored you are staying home alone with a cold or cough, home is indeed where you must stay. If you're home sick and want companionship, pick up the telephone or, if you own a computer, catch up on some e-mail.

TAKING LEAVE

It was once a fixed rule that the guest of honor should be the first to leave the party. This rule is more or less obsolete, however, unless the guest of honor is the president of the United States or other dignitary, in which case no one may leave before he or she does. In all other circumstances, other guests may depart before the guest of honor does.

When *should* a guest go home? Dinner guests should *stay at least one hour after dinner,* since it is hardly a compliment to the hostess when her guests do little more than eat and run. At a small party a couple should not leave long before anyone else seems ready to go, because their departure is very apt to break up the party.

Today it is not considered ill-mannered for any couple or individual to rise if the hour is growing late. If you are a guest, it is late, and you are ready to leave, simply stand up, say good-bye to the people with whom you were talking, say good-bye to the guest of honor, and look for your hostess. Chat for a brief moment with her and the host, and then offer your thanks and good-byes, and leave.

THE GUEST WHO NEVER LEAVES

A guest should stay as long as he wishes, within reason, while being sensitive to clues that the host and hostess and others at the party are tired. One clue is if the host announces a last call for a drink, and starts to close up the bar. Another is when the party givers start cleanup duties in earnest. There is the story of the host who, when he's ready for guests to leave, simply says good night and goes upstairs to bed. All are obvious clues that it is time to say your good-byes.

THE GLOBAL GUEST

You may be the most polished executive in your company and a confident globetrotter, but without knowing the nuances in cultural practices and customs in a foreign country it is easy to appear ignorant when you are a guest there. Differences in mores, cultural practices, decision making, and the way people converse can trip up even the most seasoned traveler. It is the wise guest who takes the time not only to understand these differences but to practice them as well. As the saying goes, when in Rome, do as the Romans do.

Here are some basic courtesies to keep in mind when you are a guest in a foreign land.

- Don't criticize the way things are done in the host country or make comparisons to your own country.

- Be prompt and punctual.
- Follow the standards of dress and grooming in the host country. Conservative is always better. In many countries, women should not wear pants, skirts above the knee, or tops that expose arms or the neckline.
- Be prepared to shake hands frequently, especially in Europe. In many countries women do not shake hands regularly; in those situations, wait for the woman to extend her arm to you for a handshake, whatever your gender.
- Show respect for older persons. Stand when they enter the room, wait for them to speak first, and wait for them to initiate a handshake.
- Do not immediately call someone by his or her first name. It's largely an American custom, so only do so when you're invited to.
- Respect your host's dietary customs; don't request something that may be offensive or contrary to his practices.

CUSTOMS AROUND THE WORLD

The following is a sampling of customs that are specific to certain countries. While the burgeoning global culture is infiltrating all corners of the globe, many traditions survive and thrive in social interaction.

Arab and Islamic Countries Never point or beckon; these gestures are reserved for summoning animals. Arabs tend to stand very close to the person to whom they are speaking. Do not distance yourself. If a handshake is accompanied by a kiss on both cheeks in social situations, return the gesture. Alcohol is forbidden and is rarely consumed in public, although it may be served at a private function. In many Arab countries, women do not dine with men, even at a business dinner, so this should be expected.

China Bow your head slightly when introduced, as a sign of respect. Speak quietly, for loud voices are considered rude. Follow your host's lead at a meal, neither eating nor drinking until he does. When a toast is given, it is practice to empty one's glass each time. If you are not used to drinking, exercise caution when toasting with an alcoholic beverage, perhaps requesting a soft drink or water instead.

France Address people formally. If you take a French host out to dinner or lunch, suggest that he select the wine, a point of pride with most French, and be sure to praise it.

Germany Handshakes are formal and are often accompanied by a barely perceptible bow, but unless one knows the host well, other touching, such as hugging or cheek kissing, is not encouraged.

Great Britain Address people formally, by title, and keep physical contact at a minimum. Handshaking is expected, but not embraces or other touching. Eat with delicacy—even small finger sandwiches are to be eaten in little bites, never popped in their entirety into the mouth.

Israel Dress in Israel is more informal than in many countries, with suit jackets left off and shirt sleeves acceptable. Understand and observe dietary restrictions, which are generally kosher; and understand religious observances, which take precedence over everything else. It is correct to say *shalom* for both hello and good-bye.

Italy When dining, plan on several courses, and know that salad is served after the main course, not before. Coffee is generally served black, so you might want to adjust your taste buds if you are used to adding milk or cream to yours.

Japan Formality is of the utmost importance; chatting or overt friendliness is not appropriate. Punctuality is also important. Handshaking is not as widely practiced as in other countries, and you should bow only if someone bows to you. Remove your shoes upon entering a Japanese home and most restaurants, placing them facing outward. If house slippers are provided, put them on. When you use the bathroom, remove the house slippers you are wearing outside the bathroom door and put on the pair outside the door that is provided to be worn into the bathroom.

Latin America Handshakes and embraces are frequent, and people stand closer together than most North Americans are used to when speaking; don't back away—it's impolite. When invited to social functions, be prepared to dine quite late.

Russia Punctuality counts in Russia, so it is a good idea to know where you are going and how long it will take you to get there.

Scandinavian countries Punctuality is important, as is privacy, and both should be respected. When offered a drink, accept it, but do not touch it until your host proposes a toast.

Spain Time and punctuality are not always adhered to, so it is a good idea to be prepared to wait and not to criticize when you are kept waiting.

When a foreign visitor who speaks little English is your guest in America, don't put him on the spot by choosing entertainments that are dependent on good language skills. Choose instead universal enjoyments like music concerts or dance performances. Even better: Bring along a friend who is proficient in your guest's language.

P O S T   N O T E S

SAYING GRACE

Q. *What should a guest do when dining with a family of another faith who says grace before meals: sit quietly or join in?*

A. A guest certainly may join in if he or she feels comfortable doing so. If your hosts ask you to join hands during the prayer, this is simply a gesture of loving friendship and in no way means you are worshipping their faith. It is not necessary for guests to make the sign of the cross themselves, however, even when their hosts do so—nor to make any gesture not practiced in the guests' own faith. If a guest chooses not to join in grace, he or she may sit (or stand) quietly until grace is finished. A clue as to whether grace is to be said is whether the hostess immediately puts her napkin in her lap. If she does not, it is a signal that she may be waiting to say grace as soon as everyone is silent.

The Good Guest

CHAPTER 19

GOOD CONVERSATION

It is not essential to be blessed with a silver tongue to be someone with whom others are delighted to talk. Conversation is an exchange of thought, not an exhibition of wit and oratory. An ability to express interest in the other person and to express your own thoughts and feelings clearly and simply is all that is required.

Conversation should be a matter of equal give and take. Unhappily, it is frequently all take. Everyone knows a nonstop talker who monopolizes each conversation, pontificating on this, opining on that, who fast gains the reputation at any gathering as a pest or a bore.

For those inclined to run on, remember this simple rule: Stop, look, and listen. In conversation, "stop" means not to rush ahead without thinking; "look" means to pay attention to the expression of the person with whom you are talking; and "listen"—meaning exactly that—is the best advice possible, because everyone loves to talk to a sympathetic listener. Remember, though, that a sympathetic listener really listens. A fixed expression of sympathy while your mind wanders far away won't fool anyone but the most self-centered conversationalist.

Watch that wandering eye, too: There is nothing more frustrating than talking to someone who is constantly looking past your shoulder, as if he is bored to tears and is searching out a more interesting situation. It is particularly rude for a man or woman to bring a date to a party and then to scour the room for new conquests while in conversation with his or her date. Keep your eyes glued to whomever you are talking with, and you will have a friend for life.

DON'T PANIC

If you dread meeting strangers because you are afraid you won't be able to think of anything to say, relax and listen. Most conversational errors are committed not by those who talk too little but by those who talk too much.

Many people do have great difficulty in carrying on a conversation. This terror is something like the terror felt by those who are learning to swim. It is not just the first stroke that overwhelms them, but the thought of all the strokes that must follow. The frightened talker doesn't hear a word that is said by others because he or she is trying so desperately to think of what to say next. So the practical rule for continuing a conversation is the same as that for swimming: Don't panic. Just take it one stroke (or word) at a time.

THINK BEFORE YOU SPEAK

Nearly all the faults or mistakes commonly made in conversation are caused by lack of consideration. For example, should a computer programmer talk in technical programming language to a professor of literature sitting next to her at dinner? Not if she realizes that as enjoyable as her work is, not everyone wishes to hear such a lengthy discourse on the subject.

By careful listening to our own words and attention to the reactions of our listeners we can discover our personal inadequacies. The burden of thinking before speaking is our own. It has been said that "I" is the smallest letter in the alphabet—so don't make it the largest word in your vocabulary.

BUT WHAT DO I TALK ABOUT?

There are those who can recount the most mundane experience to a group of people and make everyone burst into laughter. But the storyteller who constantly tries to be funny is generally a bore, and the majority of us, if we wish to be considered attractive, are safer if we rely on sincerity, clarity, and an intelligent choice of conversational subject.

Guests who are interesting and amusing can set any party afire. On the other hand, a friend who is dear to you but who makes people's eyes glaze over as she goes on and on is not someone you can count on to make your gathering sparkle with humor. While you don't want your party to consist only of a roomful of divas duking it out, you also don't want it limited to a group of wallflowers. It's all in the mix.

TALKING TO NEW ACQUAINTANCES

When you find yourself next to a stranger at a party, introduce yourself right off the bat. It is not only good manners, it is also a great help to your host or hostess. There is nothing more awkward than for guests at a party to be standing alone waiting for another to come along and perform an introduction.

The host of a small party will introduce as many people as he can. At a large affair, however, such as a wedding reception or a formal dance, it is impossible for the host to make sure that everyone has met. In these instances, it is up to you as a guest to make your own introductions.

In introducing yourself, however, never start out with, "What is your name?" Doing so is simply too abrupt. Always start by giving your own name. "Hello. I'm Amelia Coppola," you may say, extending your hand if you wish. You can also add, "I'm a friend of Judy's." If this does not elicit a response other than "Hello," you may then say "And you are. . . ?" or "And what is your name?"

If you simply want to introduce yourself to someone, by all means, go ahead. It is fine to say, for instance, "Mrs. Simms, aren't you a friend of my mother's? I'm Jane Adams, Adelaide Pinkham's daughter."

In talking to a person you have just met and about whom you know nothing, the best approach is to find a common interest. Start by referring to your host or hostess: How do you know them? Don't snatch at a period of silence in panic. Let it go for a little while. Conversation is not a race that must be continued at breakneck pace to the finish line.

DINNER-TABLE CONVERSATION

The "turning of the table" is an outdated custom designed to make people divide their conversation time more or less evenly between their two dinner companions. In the old days, the hostess, after the first two courses (or any time she chose), would turn from the man on her right to the one on her left, and each woman at the table was supposed to notice this and switch at the same time. This made something that should happen naturally into a forced act, precipitated by a signal.

Although the turning of the table is no longer a dinner-party ritual, common courtesy dictates that you must at some time during dinner talk to both your neighbors. Today, conversation at the table often includes three or four people sitting near one another. If, however, you notice that one of your neighbors is left with no one to talk to, common courtesy dictates that you should either include him in your conversation or turn at a break in your discussion to talk to him for a while.

Remember not to talk at length about yourself, but to listen to your neighbor's point of view and to avoid talking shop at great length to the exclusion of others seated near you.

Even if you imagine you have nothing in common with your neighbor and can't possibly converse, look around you. The food and wine always provide something worth talking about, as do the decor, the music, the fashions on display, and the people around you. It's all fodder for social interaction, no more complicated than connecting to people who are likely to have as much trepidation as you are in talking to strangers.

10 CONVERSATIONAL BLUNDERS

A great number of comments, especially those that are extremely personal, should be off-limits, whether you're conversing with new acquaintances or old friends. If your dinner partner wants to divulge a personal matter, he or she will initiate the conversation; it is never up to you to do so. The following are some things not to say when meeting new or old acquaintances.

1. "Why aren't you married? Why don't you have any children?"
2. "Why are you wearing that eye patch?"
3. "Are you tired? You look it." Or, even worse: "Have you had cosmetic surgery? You look so much better than you used to."
4. "How much did that cost?"
5. "You're dead wrong."
6. "How old are you? Ah, c'mon, you can tell me."
7. "That's pronounced em-PIR."
8. ". . . you know, like, I mean. . ."
9. "As the president was telling me the other day. . ."
10. "I can see I'll have to simplify this for you."

CHAPTER 20

ALL ABOUT INTRODUCTIONS

Al social events, large and small, require that those in attendance make every effort to introduce the people they are with to others they know. They need to know how to introduce themselves when joining a group, being seated at a large table with strangers, or proceeding through a receiving line.

The overall point is that one person is always introduced to another. This is achieved in one of two ways. First, by actual use of the word *to*: "Mr. King, I'd like to introduce you to Mr. Mason." Second, by saying the name of the person to *whom* the other is being introduced first, without using the preposition *to*: "Ms. Brown, may I introduce Mr. Collins?" The most important rule of all? Even if you can't recall the order of who should be introduced to whom, make the introduction anyway. To avoid doing so would be rude.

THE BASICS

There are three basic guidelines regarding introductions:

1. In social situations, a man is introduced to a woman.
   "Mrs. Pullman, I'd like you to meet Mr. Havlin."
   "Janny, this is my cousin, John Vaccaro."
   "Mr. DeRuvo, may I introduce you to my mother, Mrs. Smithson?"
   In business, the order is based on rank, not gender.

2. A young person is always introduced to an older person.
   "Dr. Josephson, I'd like you to meet my daughter, Lily Peterson."
   "Aunt Ruth, this is my roommate, Elizabeth Feeney."

3. A less prominent person is always introduced to a more important person. This rule can be complicated, since it may be difficult to determine who is more prominent. There is one guideline which may help in some circumstances: Members of your family, even though they may be more prominent, are introduced to the other person as a matter of courtesy.
   "Mr. Connor, I'd like you to meet my stepfather, Governor Bradley."
   "Mrs. Anselmi, this is my aunt, Professor Johnston."

The easiest way to not slip up is to always say the name of the woman, the older person, or the more prominent person first, followed by the phrase "I'd like you to meet . . ." or "this is . . ." or "may I introduce . . ." If you inadvertently say the wrong name first, correct your slip by saying, "Mr. Heath, I'd like to introduce you to Mrs. McGregor."

The following are some general guidelines for making introductions.

- Don't introduce people by their first names only. Always include a person's full name.
- Avoid expressing your introduction as a command, such as: "Mr. Bonner, shake hands with Mr. Heath."
- Avoid calling only one person "my friend" in an introduction, which implies that the other person is not your friend.
- Do not repeat "Mr. Jones. . . Mr. Smith. Mr. Smith. . . Mr. Jones." To say each name once is enough.

THE "NONINTRODUCTION"

Sometimes it happens that in talking to one person, you want to include another in your conversation without making an introduction. Suppose you are talking in your yard to a gardener, and a friend joins you. You greet her and then casually include her by saying, "Mr. Smith is suggesting that I dig up these daisies and put in delphiniums." Whether or not your friend makes any comment, she has been made part of your conversation.

SO, YOU'VE BEEN INTRODUCED. . . NOW WHAT?

Just as you give a person who is being introduced to you your undivided attention, you look a person to whom you are being introduced to in the eye and greet him or her cordially. Repeating the person's name—"Hello, Dr. Shine, it's certainly a pleasure to meet you"—is a technique that helps you remember the name and is a sign that you are, indeed, paying attention to the introduction. It's also very flattering to the person being introduced.

WHEN INCORRECTLY INTRODUCED

We have all, at one time or another, been incorrectly introduced. A title may be wrongly given, a name confused or mispronounced, an identification completely off base. It is only sensible and kind that the person being introduced corrects the error immediately. If, for example, a hostess introduces a general practitioner to a group as "a surgeon who has just moved to Greenwich," he should explain this to the new acquaintances—and the hostess, if she remains there—at once. He should also make a correction should she refer to him as "Mr." instead of "Dr.," or call him "Dr. Donald" instead of "Dr. McDonald."

When someone is introducing a stranger to a number of people and consistently says the name wrong, the person being introduced should correct the host as soon as he realizes it is not just a slip of the tongue. He should do so not with annoyance, but by making light of it. All he need say is, "I know it's confusing, but my name is 'Light,' not 'Bright,' " or "Actually, it's Frances, not Francesca."

If you are introduced by your correct name and someone immediately finds a diminutive or nickname for you, you may say, "Would you mind calling me Jeffrey? For some reason, I've never been called Jeff." If the other person insists on his own version, you may correct him one more time and, after that, just ignore his discourtesy the best that you can.

WHEN YOU DON'T USE FIRST NAMES

On occasion, you should not use first names in introductions. When meeting one of the following people first names may not be used except when they request it.

- A person of higher rank (a diplomat, a public official, a professor, for example)
- Professional people offering you their services (doctors, lawyers, and so on). In turn, they should not use your first name unless you request them to.
- An older person, such as an adult to a child.

HOW AND WHEN TO SHAKE HANDS

A handshake between two strangers can create an immediate impression, ranging from warm friendliness to instant irritation. A "boneless" hand that feels like a limp glove is as big a turnoff as a viselike grasp that temporarily paralyzes every finger. The proper handshake is brief but firm and warm. It should always be accompanied by a direct look into the eyes of the person whose hand you are grasping. Traditionally, shaking hands occurs when people are introduced to one another or when they meet acquaintances on the street, at a function or social occasion, or in business situations. As in introductions, there is a protocol for this form of greeting.

- A child should be prepared to shake hands when introduced to adults who offer their hands to him or her.
- When a man is introduced to a woman, she smiles and says, "Hello" or "How do you do?" Traditionally speaking, in social situations, it is her place to offer her hand or not, as she chooses, but if he should extend his hand, she must give him hers. Nothing could be ruder than to ignore spontaneous friendliness.
- An older person extends his or her hand first to a younger one.
- A "more important" person offers his or her hand to a "less important" person.
- When you meet someone whose right arm or hand is missing or disabled, extend your right hand even though he or she cannot shake hands in the normal way. The disabled person will appreciate that you have made no unnatural gesture to accommodate his or her problem. He or she will respond by offering his or her left hand, or by saying, "Please forgive me if I don't shake hands, but I'm very glad to meet you."
- If you are disabled or are suffering an injury or illness such as arthritis and it is impossible or painful for you to shake hands, you shouldn't feel you must. Simply say, as noted above, "I'm so glad to meet you; please forgive me for not shaking hands. I have arthritis [or a sprained finger or whatever the trouble may be]."

WHEN A GUEST IS UNKNOWN TO THE HOSTESS

When you bring a guest that no one knows to a party, remember to introduce him or her to everyone you possibly can. You don't have to make a grand tour of the room, but it is unfair to expect your hostess to look after *your* guest and have a stranger's name at the tip of her tongue all evening long.

WHEN TO RISE

Hosts and hostesses always rise to greet each arriving guest. Members of the hosts' family, including young people, also rise as a guest enters the room, although they do not all necessarily shake hands, with this exception: A young-ster who is sitting and chatting with an adult need not rise as each new guest comes in. He should stand up instantly, however, if the guest is brought over to be introduced.

A woman does not stand when being introduced to someone at a distance. Nor need she rise when shaking hands with anyone, unless that person is much older, very prominent, someone she has wanted to meet for some time, or is someone with whom she wants to go on talking. In the first case, think before you leap. Some women would hardly feel complimented if a woman only a few years younger were to jump up for them.

In a social situation, a man should rise when a woman comes into a room *for the first time* and remain standing until she is seated or leaves his vicinity. He does not jump up every time a hostess or another guest goes in and out. A hus-band rises for his wife when she comes in after they have been apart for a time. This is not a matter of manners but simply of saying, "I'm glad to see you."

IN RECEIVING LINES

If the reception or party is a large celebration for a guest of honor, the hostess receives, standing with the special guest. As each guest approaches, the hostess says, "Mrs. Famous, this is my neighbor, Mrs. Johnson"; "Mr. Prominent, our headmaster, Dr. Riley"; or simply "Mrs. Notable, Mrs. Stokes." The guest of honor offers his or her hand, and the other guest says, "How do you do?" or "I'm so glad to meet you," and moves on. A receiving line is never the place to conduct a prolonged conversation or say anything more than "How do you do?" "I'm so pleased to meet you," or any other brief greeting.

When an invited guest has brought guests of her own to the reception, she precedes them in the line and introduces them to the hostess, who in turn intro-duces her and her guests to the guest of honor.

On formal occasions when (as a guest) you do not know any of the people in the line, nor could they be expected to know you, you introduce yourself for-mally: "I am Charles Smith," or a woman would say, "I am Janet Smith" and, turning to her husband behind her, "and this is my husband, Charles Smith."

Introductions are always required when a guest of honor is presented to other guests. If you arrive after the receiving line has dispersed, you must introduce yourself; it is considered rude to attend a party given in honor of someone and fail to say "How do you do?" to him.

At a smaller, more casual party given for someone known to most of the people present, the guest of honor does not receive with the hostess but sits or stands in a convenient place so that everyone can go up and talk to him or her. Whether there is a receiving line or not, a woman introduces herself as "Janet Smith" and her husband as "my husband, Bob." If she is escorted by a person who is not her husband she would introduce herself and say, "and this is Douglas Jones."

INTRODUCTIONS AT A FORMAL DINNER

Strangers sitting next to each other at the table should introduce themselves, using one's full name, such as "I'm Arthur Robinson." Your neighbor's place card is a handy reminder if you do not quite catch, or do not remember, the name he or she has given you.

Whether you exchange names or not, you must accept the obligation of talking to the person you are seated next to at the dinner table. To sit side by side without speaking is a great discourtesy to the hostess, as well as to the person you have been ignoring. Equally rude: Devoting all your time to the person on one side of you and ignoring the guest on the other.

SPECIAL CASES

When introducing family members, it is not necessary to specify the relationship, but it is helpful to include an identifying phrase. This provides a conversational opening for strangers. Since you courteously give precedence to the other person when introducing a family member, the identifying phrase comes at the end of the introduction: "Mrs. Cottrell, I'd like you to meet my daughter, Deborah."

How does one introduce his or her live-in companion? Although you usually identify family members as such, you needn't identify boyfriends, girlfriends, or live-in companions with their relationship to you. Saying his or her name is sufficient.

Children, when introducing their parents, use first names depending on to whom they are making the introduction. One should always use the name that the newly introduced pair will use in talking to one another. If you are introducing your roommate to your father, he would, of course, call your father by the title "Mr." If you are introducing your roommate's father to your father, you would use your father's full name: "Mr. Davies, may I introduce my father, Franklin Palmer?

POST NOTES

FAULTY MEMORY

Q. *I often forget people's names and am at a loss to introduce them to others. How can I make introductions under these situations?*

A. There is nothing you can do but introduce the friend who has joined you to the person whose name you've forgotten by saying to the latter, "Oh, do you know Janet McCall?" Hopefully the nameless person will be tactful and understanding enough to announce his own name. If he doesn't, and your friend makes matters worse by saying, "You didn't tell me his name," it's even more embarrassing. The only solution is to be completely frank, admit you're having a mental block, and ask them to complete the introduction themselves.

Remember the feeling, however, and when you meet someone who obviously doesn't remember your name or might not remember it, offer it at once. Say immediately, "Hello, I'm Julie Hopewell. I met you at the Andersons' last Christmas." Never say, "You don't remember me, do you?"—which only embarrasses the other person.

CHAPTER 21

GIFT ETIQUETTE

GIFTS FOR THE HOST AND HOSTESS

The more personal the gift, the more sincere and thoughtful—and the more thoughtful, the more meaningful to your host. An expensive, elaborate gift is not necessarily the right choice as a gesture of thanks from a guest to his host or hostess.

First, always consider the nature of the occasion before you bring a gift. The gift you give to a weekend host should be grander than the one you take to a dinner party host. In the event of a cocktail party or open house, it is not necessary to take the host a gift at all. Second, always make sure you aren't simply giving the host one more thing to be responsible for. Flowers, wine, and food are all excellent gifts but can present their own set of problems. Flowers brought to a dinner party obligate an already busy hostess to find a vase and arrange them. Solve that by putting your flowers in a vase. A small plant or floral arrangement eliminates the problem altogether.

Unless you have consulted with your dinner-party hostess about bringing a contribution toward the dinner, don't bring food as a gift. When a dinner guest arrives at the door with an apple pie that was not mentioned in advance, instead of feeling overjoyed, the hostess is often put on the spot. She feels an obligation to serve it, to share it with the other guests. This is fine if no dessert has been made or if it can be served with the dessert the hostess has prepared. If, however, the sideboard is groaning with desserts, the hostess should, of course, be tactful, warmly thanking her guest for the apple pie while putting it aside to save for later. Remember: Guests who have not cleared their intentions with their hostess beforehand shouldn't be hurt if their unexpected gift is not immediately used. The hostess should feel free to use it as she wishes.

If you do bring a gift of food, make it clear that the item is not intended for the meal being served (unless, of course, the host or hostess chooses to serve them). Instead, stress that the gift of croissants and jam is "for your breakfast tomorrow," a bottle of champagne is "for your next special quiet time together," or a box of cookies is "for the children to enjoy tomorrow." All are thoughtful gift ideas.

When party givers are presented with not one but two or three unexpected dessert offerings, it is not unreasonable to cut into, or open, all of them, so they should choose the one that seems to go best with the meal and appeals most to the guests—that is, if the host wants to offer these gifts at all.

The custom of taking wine as a gift to a small dinner party has become widespread. It is not too expensive or elaborate and can be shelved for later use by the host. Wrapped in a pretty wrapping—colored tissue paper tied up with ribbon, for example—a bottle of wine is indeed a festive gift. Again, the host has no obligation to serve it with dinner. The host should thank the donor and tell him how much he'll enjoy the gift at another meal.

Ordinarily, neither a gift sent later nor a note is necessary for a dinner-party invitation; your verbal thanks when you leave is enough. A phone call the next day—or even a note—to say how much you enjoyed the evening is always welcome.

Gifts need not be taken to large formal dinners, especially if you don't know the guests well, unless it is to honor a special occasion. It may not be customary among your hosts' other dinner party guests to bring a gift, and you will only embarrass those who have not brought one. If you're the guest of honor, however, you should send flowers to your hostess before or on the day of the party or give her another gift if you think she would prefer it to flowers.

In some areas a gift is taken to a host or hostess who has extended an invitation to an evening out, a restaurant and the theater, for example. In other localities gifts are not expected. In Europe it is customary to take cut flowers to a hostess, and if you do not do so, you should send flowers with a thank-you card the next day. This is also much appreciated in our own country.

If a wrapped gift is brought to a dinner party, it is a nice touch for the hostess to open it in front of the person who brought it. But she should do so without fanfare, so that she doesn't embarrass other guests who did not bring gifts. If the hostess has no time to do this, a verbal thank you to the donor within the next few days is sufficient. A hostess is not obliged to send a thank-you note for her own hostess gift—it is a gift meant as thanks to the hosts.

Gifts For a Weekend Visit

Houseguests who stay a weekend or longer should always send or take a gift for their host and/or hostess. You may send flowers in advance or along with the thank-you note after you leave. You may bring a gift with you, a bottle of special wine, perhaps, or some homemade delicacy. Also welcome: a pretty country bowl or pitcher; candles and candleholders; cookbooks; linen napkins; or some foodstuff your hosts cannot find where they live.

The choice of gift often hinges on the length of the visit and the elaborateness of the entertainment. You may take the host and hostess to dinner or to another entertainment, or take the fixings for one evening's meal, which you prepare and serve as a thank you for their hospitality. Be sure to let your hosts know ahead of time, however, so they won't make conflicting plans.

Weekend guests from out of town can easily send flowers by making an order over the phone or on the Internet from the comfort of their home and having them delivered to a distant town or city by an associated florist there. Those who find it cumbersome to shop for a gift need only pick up the telephone and make a call to give pleasure to someone far away.

Gifts for Housewarmings

A guest invited to a housewarming generally takes a small gift that need not be expensive. In lieu of the ubiquitous bouquet of flowers, however, which last but a brief few days, you might want to give something more permanent. Always welcome are guest towels, place mats, houseplants, glasses, linen dishcloths or napkins, and garden bulbs and seeds.

If the housewarming is for new neighbors from far away, anything that will help them orient themselves to the neighborhood and surrounding area is bound to be appreciated. Gather together a local road map, local transportation schedules, brochures on local activities and points of interest, registration forms for pet licenses, parking permits—anything you can think of that will make moving in easier and make your new neighbors feel welcome and at home.

1. Take a photograph of your friends in front of their new home. Have a print made, then frame and wrap it.

2. Create a keepsake with an attractive guest book. Place it at the door of the new house and have all the guests sign it, adding comments, addresses, and phone numbers. Present it to the hosts at the end of the party.

3. Put together, with several other neighbors, if you wish, an old-fashioned welcome-wagon–style basket of staples a homeowner can't do without. A beribboned basket full of nails, notepads, a screwdriver, tape, a corkscrew—even a toilet plunger—makes a fun and useful offering.

4. Have each of your neighbors prepare a casserole that can be frozen to give to the new neighbor to thaw and cook when busy with unpacking and renovating.

5. Give personalized return address labels of the new address.

6. Put together jars of fresh spices by visiting a store that sells freshly ground spices in bulk and buying four to six empty glass jars. Fill the jars and place handwritten labels on each.

7. Present an address book listing the names, addresses, and phone numbers of recommended local services and stores.

8. Give a subscription to the local newspaper of the new town or area.

9. Prepare a basket full of garden bulbs and seeds.

10. Present discount coupons to local movie theaters, restaurants, and shops.

GIFTS FOR ALL OCCASIONS

ANNIVERSARY PARTIES

The question of whether or not to bring gifts to an anniversary couple is often answered on the invitation itself. Many couples celebrating a milestone anniversary often include a "No gifts" written request on the invitation. Among the loveliest ways to say "No gifts" was mentioned in a letter to advice columnist Ann Landers. The letter dealt with a simple yet elegant way to request no gifts on the occasion of a 50th wedding anniversary:

> *Mr. and Mrs. William Carson*
> *invite relatives and friends to attend*
> *a worship service and reception*
> *honoring*
> *Elizabeth and Daniel Bailey*
> *in celebration of their 50th wedding anniversary.*
> *Your love and friendship are cherished gifts.*
> *We respectfully request no other.*

For couples who do not want personal gifts, there is another solution. The persons giving the party should enclose a note with the invitation that says, "In place of gifts, please, if you wish, send a contribution to Mom and Dad's favorite charity—the XYZ Research Foundation." Guests who do so should send a check with a note saying, "Please accept this contribution in honor of the 50th anniversary of Mr. and Mrs. John Doe."

No one giving a 25th-anniversary party should ever write "No silver" or "No silver gifts, please." That is simply a clear hint that while the couple does not want silver they do expect other gifts.

Nor is it ever proper for a hostess to request a gift of money for herself. A couple giving their own anniversary party cannot, in good taste, suggest to their friends that they would like gifts of cash. In most circumstances it is incorrect to include a request for money on the invitation to an anniversary celebration. If, however, the people giving the party have planned a special group present such as tickets for a cruise, a new television set, or a fine painting, it's proper to enclose a short note with the invitation explaining what has been planned and asking the guests if they would like to make a contribution in place of bringing an individual gift. Each guest who contributes should sign the card accompanying the gift.

If you do bring a gift, remember that it doesn't have to be composed of the traditional material allotted to each anniversary. But because many people feel that the gift is more meaningful if it is a traditional one, the following list, modified in some cases to include modern materials, offers suggestions. When an article of the original material cannot be purchased, something similar but not identical may be chosen—for example, a stainless-steel or pewter platter instead of a silver one on a 25th anniversary. For all anniversaries, a lovely flower arrangement or a plant that can be set out in the couple's garden is almost always appropriate.

	TRADITIONAL, AND MODIFIED, ANNIVERSARY GIFT MATERIALS	SUGGESTED GIFTS
1	PAPER OR PLASTICS	*Books, notepaper, magazine or newspaper subscriptions*
2	CALICO OR COTTON	*Cotton napkins and place mats, cotton throw, tapestries*
3	LEATHER OR SIMULATED LEATHER	*Photo album, leather bag or suitcase*
4	SILK OR SYNTHETIC MATERIAL	*Silk flowers, silk handkerchiefs or scarf*
5	WOOD	*Picture frames, hand-painted wooden trays, wicker baskets*
6	IRON	*Fireplace tool set, windchimes*
7	COPPER OR WOOL	*Copper bowls, pots or kettle; wool afghan*
8	ELECTRICAL APPLIANCES	*Hand mixer, blender, waffle maker, espresso maker*
9	POTTERY	*Ceramic vase, platter, pitcher, bowl*
10	TIN OR ALUMINUM	*Pretty cookie or biscuit tins, mailbox*
11	STEEL	*Stainless-steel kitchen utensils or bowls*
12	LINEN	*Damask tablecloth*
13	LACE	*Textiles*
14	FORMERLY IVORY, NOW ENDANGERED	*Jewelry*
15	CRYSTAL OR GLASS	*Christmas ornaments, champagne, carafe*
20	CHINA	*Hand-painted bowl, platter*
25	SILVER	*Ice bucket, wine bucket*
30	PEARLS	*Pearl-handled steak knives*
35	FORMERLY CORAL, NOW ENDANGERED	*Brooches, figurines*
40	RUBY	*Jewelry*
45	SAPPHIRE	*Jewelry*
50	GOLD	*Gold-leaf stationery, jewelry*
55	EMERALD	*Jewelry*
60	DIAMOND	*Jewelry*
70	DIAMOND	*Jewelry*
75	DIAMOND	*Jewelry*

Other ways to honor the anniversary couple:

- Enlist the aid of the couple's relatives to gather photos of the couple and their family taken over the course of their marriage. Arrange the photos in a collage-type frame, perhaps leaving a space blank to insert a photo from the anniversary party.
- Offer to videotape or photograph the party.
- Give a photo album (to be filled later, if possible, with pictures taken at the party) or a framed family portrait.
- Pass around a blank writing album at the party and ask longtime friends and relatives to write a message or anecdote about the couple.
- Present a book related to the couple's hobbies or interests.

BABY SHOWERS

Babies grow by leaps and bounds, and any article of clothing is always a welcome present for new parents. Other useful items include blankets and comforters; even towels and washcloths come in handy. Close relatives might consider a silver fork and spoon, or even baby's first piggy bank. If you are imaginative, personalize a scrapbook with the baby's birth date and all pertinent information, and fill the first few pages with photos of the parents, grandparents, and baby's first home. Include the newspaper and horoscope from the day the baby was born.

It is always thoughtful for a close friend or relative attending a shower to take a big brother or sister a small gift. It is hard enough for young children to learn to share Mommy or Daddy, let alone see piles of presents being given to the interloper!

BIRTHDAY GIFTS FOR GROWN-UPS

When adults throw birthday parties or any other kind of informal celebration for themselves that require a gift, it's perfectly appropriate to present a humorous gag gift instead of a "real" gift. You must first gauge the informality of the party and whether participants are close friends—because it can be embarrassing when gifts are opened and yours is the only offbeat "over the hill" present among luxury items given by everyone else. If you are not certain which direction to take, call others invited to the party to gauge what kinds of gifts they are bringing.

Religious Ceremonies for Newborns

Those invited to a christening or *bris* usually take a gift to the baby because they are presumably close to the family. The gift should be a lasting memento of the occasion and thus is often engraved. Typical gifts include a silver picture frame or a silver comb and brush set.

Godparents give the baby as nice a present as they can afford. The typical gift is a silver mug or porringer, inscribed, for example:

ERIC DEGENHARDT

JULY 6, 1999

FROM HIS GODFATHER

MARVIN HENK

Other typical presents are a silver fork and spoon, a government bond, or a trust fund to which the donor may add each year until the child is grown. Other appropriate gifts are books, toys, and clothing.

Religious Confirmation, First Communion, Bar or Bat Mitzvah

Any of the following are acceptable: prayer book, religious charm or pendant, a gift of money, jewelry, a fine book, or a pen-and-pencil set. Select your gift based on your closeness to the youngster. From other young people, gift certificates for music, clothing, video stores, and fitness centers, as well as sports equipment, are appropriate, depending on the age of the recipient.

Sweet-16 and Graduation Parties

Birthday gifts for a sweet-16 party are generally in the category of gift certificates to a favorite clothes, music, or video store; a fashion magazine subscription; personalized stationery; jewelry; perfume; a scarf, belt, or other fashion accessory; cassettes or CDs.

For teenage boys, clothing, sports equipment, and CDs are generally good choices. Other ideas include video games, computer software, coupons to a local movie theater, or a fitness center gift certificate.

BON VOYAGE PARTIES

Expensive, elaborate gifts at a bon voyage party are unnecessary—the occasion is really just an excuse to share in the giddy celebration of seeing friends off on a travel adventure. Small, useful travel-oriented items are more appropriate gifts: guidebooks, a trip diary, a travel reading light, a passport folder, a money-exchange guide, or a kit of travel-size toiletries and cleaning products. If the guests of honor are taking a cruise, arrange with the wine steward to have champagne or wine served as a surprise during the voyage. Most travelers would welcome a supply of extra film, but a special treat is including the pre-paid processing mailer that allows travelers to be greeted by their photos when they return home.

Every traveler needs a certain amount of small-denomination bills and loose change for tips and cab fare when he first arrives at his destination. One way in which to do so is to give the traveler the equivalent of 20 dollars' worth of bills and change in the currency of the country he is visiting. This thoughtfulness speeds travelers through airport and hotel check-in without their having to take time to exchange money. For those traveling with electric hair dryers or traveling irons, a set of electric-current converter plugs is a handy gift.

GLOBAL GIFT GIVING

The giving of gifts internationally varies from country to country. You would be wise to find out ahead of time what kinds of gifts are appropriate—and *when* it is appropriate to give them. A gift purchased in your home country before your trip is often more appreciated than one bought in the country you are visiting. Gifts from well-known North American stores or chains, distinctly American nonperishable foods and products with logos from popular U.S. sports teams, are some smart choices. Don't go overboard, however, with a gift that is too ostentatious or expensive.

Most important, make sure you aren't committing a terrible breach of etiquette by presenting a gift that is offensive to your host. You would never give a gift of cowhide in India, for example, where the cow is considered sacred. You would not present a gift of flowers in Japan, as flowers there are given only in the event of courtship, illness, or death.

Timing is important as well. In Middle Eastern countries and in Japan, you should not be the first to present a gift, as this causes your host to lose face.

Wait instead for the host to give you a gift or token, and be prepared to reciprocate immediately and in kind. In Russia, gifts are often given at a dinner during toasts but rarely in an office or conference room.

When visiting the home of your host in another country, you should bring gifts for any children in the house. For the host, a gift of flowers or chocolates is entirely appropriate, while a bottle of wine or liquor may not be. It depends on the local customs and what you know about your host's personal preferences.

Certain flowers often have symbolic meaning in other countries; before selecting a bouquet for your host, find out whether the flowers you choose are appropriate. White flowers, for example, are symbols of mourning in the Far East, as are gladiolus and chrysanthemums in many other countries. Yellow flowers have negative connotations in Peru, Mexico, and Iran, where they are associated with hate or mourning.

If you choose cut flowers, have the florist send them early enough that your host has time to arrange them before you arrive.

Finally, when you arrive for a meal or an overnight stay, by all means compliment the host on his home, his children, and the food served—just as you would hope to receive compliments in your own home.

CHAPTER 22

A WINE PRIMER

The fizz in a party can be enhanced by a convivial cocktail or a glass of wine. While an overload of alcohol can quickly "de-fizz" a joyous occasion, wine with dinner is one of the great pleasures of communing with friends; used with taste and decorum, wine or champagne nicely complements and balances the flavors of a meal. And these days, it is no secret that drinking wine in moderation with meals is good for the heart and for the digestion.

Many novice hosts consider choosing a wine to be a daunting proposition. It doesn't have to be; simply ask your local wine merchant for advice. And be sure to taste before you buy. Most of the time, the wine that tastes best to you will also taste great to your guests. Although the tradition of serving a particular wine with a particular food is no longer de rigueur, the fact remains that red wines nicely complement a bold sauce or a hearty roast pork, while white and rosé wines neatly balance chicken and seafood dishes. Of course, unless the meal is strictly formal there is no reason why the host may not choose any wine he thinks his guests would prefer. A Beaujolais, for example, often complements a heavier, oilier fish. The two most important considerations in choosing a wine are not the cost or where it came from, but that its flavors complement the food with which it is served and that it pleases the palates of the people drinking it.

Here are some basic tips on serving and enjoying wine.

- If more than one wine is to be served during dinner, set a glass for each wine.
- The general rule in serving several types of wine is whites before reds, dry before sweet.
- Don't "fill 'er up": When pouring wine, fill the wineglass only halfway, never to the top of the glass, to allow the wine to breathe.

- Pick up your wineglass by the stem rather than the bowl. In the case of white wine and champagne this helps keep the wine cool. In the case of all wines, including red wines, holding the glass by the stem lets you better appreciate the color.
- If you're serving wine at a dinner party, plan on buying at least one bottle of wine per every two guests. Of course, this is dependent on the number of people you know will drink wine with dinner and your estimate of how much they usually drink.
- Once a bottle is opened, the wine should be drunk within a day or so—oxidation causes wine to rapidly deteriorate. To give wine a couple more days of drinkability, you might pour it into a smaller bottle or use one of several new gadgets that actually pump the air out of the bottle, creating a vacuum. Otherwise, use leftover wine in cooking.
- When buying wine, shop around. Prices can vary greatly from one wine store to another. Look for specials in your local newspaper. Many stores offer a discount (generally 10 percent) when you buy by the case (12 bottles per case). If you find you like a particular wine, you might want to consider buying it at a good price, by the case. Another way to buy good wine at reduced prices is to go to the source. Wineries are cropping up in most regions of the country, and visiting one on a tasting tour makes for a fine weekend excursion.
- Store wine bottles in a cool, dark place, preferably on their sides.

APERITIFS

Aperitifs include Lillet, Dubonnet, Campari, Cinzano, dry or sweet vermouths, and sherry. They are generally offered as a before-meal choice along with other cocktails, but sherry may also be the first wine offered at dinner and can also be served at lunch or supper.

Sherry is generally served from a decanter at room temperature and poured into small, V-shape glasses. If you don't have sherry glasses, small wineglasses or liqueur glasses are suitable substitutes. Sherry can stand being decanted almost indefinitely without spoiling.

Other aperitifs are served according to preference, either in small old-fashioned glasses with ice, or chilled or at room temperature in a small aperitif glass.

WHITE WINE

White wines should be served chilled—around 45°F—but never ice cold, which tends to overwhelm the taste. Chilling can take place in the refrigerator for a couple of hours before serving, or wine may be cooled in a bucket or cooler

filled with a mixture of ice and cold water. (Some whites, such as Chardonnays, can be chilled in less than two hours before serving.) The actual melting of the ice in the water will cool the wine faster than if it is immersed in cracked ice alone. If you live in a cold-weather region, try using snow instead of ice in your bucket; it's an eye-pleasing way to chill white wines. Drawing the cork and turning the bottle from time to time will hasten the cooling.

Traditionally, white wines were served with white meats such as fish and chicken and with fruit and salads. This custom has become more relaxed, since many people drink white wine as their cocktail and prefer to continue drinking it throughout the meal, no matter what the entrée is. Unlike red wine, white wine contains no sediment; therefore, the bottle may be upended to empty it.

Serve white wine in tulip-shaped, stemmed glasses.

RED WINE

Red wines, for the most part, are served at a cool room temperature, preferably the same temperature it would be if kept in a wine cellar—approximately 60°F to 65°F. If your wine is too cool, warm it by placing your hands around the bowl of the glass, or by leaving it out at room temperature at least 10 minutes before serving.

Traditionally, full-bodied red wines are served with beef, lamb, and robust pasta sauces—although, as with white, red wines are often drunk regardless of the entrée as a wine of preference. This is particularly true if you are serving a light red wine, such as a Beaujolais.

Serve red wines in round-bowled, stemmed glasses that are wider at the rim than white-wine glasses.

Rosé wines of the nonsparkling variety are in the red wine family but should be served very chilled. They nicely complement lighter entrées such as fish, veal, chicken, and fruit.

SPARKLING WINES

The sparklers, which shine at celebrations of all sorts, come in many forms, from the sparkling white wine known as champagne to sparkling rosé wines and sparkling burgundies.

Champagne, above all other beverages, is emblematic of a very special occasion. When other wines are included, champagne is generally served with the meat course, but when it is the only wine it is served as soon as the first course has begun. Its proper temperature depends upon its quality. Only the sparkling wines that are made in the Champagne district of France are true Champagnes. Champagnes made from American-grown grapes are labeled "méthode Champagne."

Champagne of nonvintage quality can be placed in the refrigerator for a day and then chilled further in a cooler filled with ice and a pinch or two of salt. Occasionally hold the bottle by the neck and turn it back and forth a few times. Take care not to leave the bottle in the salt and ice for a long time, or the champagne may be transformed to sherbet; check it regularly. When opening, be sure to wrap the bottle in a towel or napkin as protection in case the cork ejects too fast and champagne spills over.

An excellent vintage champagne, on the other

LEFT: *Flute*
BELOW: *Coupe*

hand, ideally should be packed in ice without salt, which chills it just a little less.

There are two shapes of champagne glasses, *coupe*-shaped and flutes. *Coupe*-shaped glasses generally have hollow stems, which cause the champagne to warm because of the heat of the fingers holding the stem. A flute tends to prolong the life of the effervescent bubbles that distinguish champagne from other wines.

Ideally, champagne glasses should be as thin as soap bubbles. Thick glasses raise the temperature at which a really fine champagne should be served and spoil its perfection. If you only have thick glasses on hand, keep them chilled in the refrigerator until the moment the champagne is to be poured.

DESSERT WINES

After-dinner drinks, such as cognac or Frangelica, are served at room temperature and often accompany coffee. Sauternes and other sweet wines are generally served with dessert, chilled.

For glasses, you'll need:

1. Brandy snifters, either large or small, to serve cognac or Armagnac
2. Small, stemmed glasses for sweet liqueurs
3. Regular wineglasses to serve port
4. Small old-fashioned glasses for white or green crème de menthe to be served over cracked ice.

THE PLACEMENT OF GLASSES

If you are serving a variety of wines with dinner, glasses are generally arranged according to size so that the smaller ones are not hidden behind the larger ones. The water goblet is placed directly above the knives at the right of the plate. The champagne glass is next to it at a slight distance to the right. The red or white wineglass is positioned in front of and between the water goblet and champagne glass. If you have several wineglasses, always set them according to size, with the largest ones on the left, starting with the water goblet. The sherry glass is placed either to the right or in front of the wineglass.

If you don't want to group the wineglasses, place them in a straight row

slanting downward from the water goblet at the upper left to the sherry glass at the lower right.

SERVING WINE

First of all, have the water glasses filled just before the guests enter the dining room or as soon as they are seated. After all of the water glasses are filled, you may then serve the wine. An opened bottle is placed on the table in front of the host, preferably on a coaster or wine holder to prevent any drops from soiling the tablecloth. If there are several guests, a second bottle is placed at the other end of the table and the host asks the person at that end to assist him in pouring.

If the dinner party has a wait staff, servers should go to the right side of each guest and quietly ask whether he or she would care for wine. Glasses are then filled from the right—and should never be lifted up from the table to meet the bottle. If more than one wine is being served the host should instruct the servers ahead of time, if necessary, which glasses are to be used for which wine. During the dinner or the serving of a course, a server keeps an eye on each guest's glass and carefully refills it when he sees it is empty.

If you don't want wine, simply say, "No, thank you" when the server comes around. Never cover your glass with your hand or turn the glass upside down to indicate that you are not partaking.

It's All in the Grape

Most of the fine wines in the world are made from a select group of grapes, called "noble" grapes for their sterling pedigree. The names below are among the most familiar wines in most restaurants and wine stores around the country.

GRAPE	DESCRIPTION	COMPLEMENTS
RED		
CABERNET SAUVIGNON	This popular grape makes a dry, tannin-rich wine and some of the most prestigious reds in the world.	*Beef, lamb, heavier fish*
MERLOT	A very popular wine these days, merlot is a smoother, softer version of Cabernet Sauvignon.	*Beef, pasta with tomato sauce, cream sauces*
PINOT NOIR	The only Red Burgundy grape. Lighter in color than Cabernet Sauvignon and Merlot.	*Rich, oily fish like salmon or bluefish*
WHITE		
CHARDONNAY	Full, ripe, and fruity; when aged in oak barrels can have an oaky taste	*Chicken, rice, pasta*
SAUVIGNON BLANC	Crisp, dry wine, with either citric or grassy undertones	*Fish, shellfish, vegetables*
RIESLING	Slightly sweeter than either Chardonnay or Sauvignon Blanc	*Lighter fish, pork tenderloin, fruits*

WHEN THE WINE IS VERY FINE

These days, most wines are ready to drink when you buy them. But if you come into possession of a fine vintage red wine that has spent some time in a cellar aging, give it the attention it deserves. A good wine needs to be handled with a little care for its excellence to be fully appreciated.

Fancy vintage reds that are stored on their sides for years form a sediment on one side of the bottle. A day or two before you are to drink it, remove the wine from the wine cellar or closet and stand it up to let the sediment settle at the bottom. If you don't have time to let the bottle stand for a day, serve it in a wine cradle or basket, letting the bottle rest at a 45-degree angle.

Plan to leave the bottle open an hour or so before you serve it to give the wine an opportunity to breathe and rid itself of any musty or other unpleasant odor it might have developed in the cellar. Don't let a fine old wine breathe too much, however: You can let in so much air that the wine will be oxidized—ruined—before you drink it. Two to three hours, tops, is all the time needed for vintage reds to breathe.

When you open the bottle, cut the foil neatly away to prevent the wine from coming in contact with it while it is being poured. For the same reason, a damp cloth is used to wipe the mouth of the bottle, to remove any accumulated residue. The cork is then carefully pulled and placed beside the neck of the bottle in its basket so that the host or any interested guest may note that it is undamaged.

Take care when pouring the wine to avoid any backlash or bubbling that can agitate the sediment resting in the bottom of the bottle. Do not pour the last inch or so in the bottle, since this will be murky with sediment.

When a bottle of red wine is so heavy with sediment that the procedure above will not result in a palatable drink, it may be decanted.

CHAPTER 23

MEALTIME MANNERS

Many a budding executive has been passed over for a promotion because his or her table manners were less than desirable. His job performance may have been exemplary, but the minute he waved his fork in the air to make a point or talked with a mouth full of food, he signaled to superiors that his table manners were lacking—making him a poor candidate to deal with clients or work with senior management.

Consideration for others is the rule governing good table manners. It's unappetizing for other diners to see someone talking at full gallop with food in his mouth, making noises while eating, or creating a mess of his food. Scraping and dragging chairs or rattling knives and forks against the plate only annoys those seated nearby.

Table manners should be practiced at home. When always used in private, they will always be used in public.

Whether you're seated across the dinner table from a U.S. senator or your host's 15-year-old son, show that person respect by demonstrating good table manners. Here is a guide to some of the most common situations you'll face at the dinner table.

MANNERS AT THE TABLE

The question always arises about the correct way to use a knife and fork. The American custom of "zigzag" eating (changing the fork from the left to the right hand after cutting) is perfectly correct. The knife is put down on the plate after cutting and the fork is raised to the mouth, tines up. Equally correct is the European method of leaving the fork in the left hand after cutting and raising it to the mouth in the same position in which is was held for cutting, tines down. The knife may also be used as a "pusher" if necessary. To do so, hold the knife in the left hand in the same position as when cutting with the right hand, and use the tip of the blade to help guide and push the food onto the fork.

When the main course is finished, the knife and fork are placed beside each other on the dinner plate diagonally from upper left to lower right, the handles extended slightly over the edge of the plate. The dessert spoon and/or fork is placed in the same position on the plate when the diner has finished. If dessert is served in a stemmed or deep bowl on another plate, the dessert spoon is put down on the plate, never left in the bowl. If the bowl is shallow and wide, the spoon may be left in it or on the plate below it, as you wish.

Ideal posture at the table is to sit straight, but not stiffly, leaning slightly against the back of the chair. When you are not actually eating, your hands may lie in your lap, which will automatically prevent you from fussing with implements. Hands should also be kept away from the face, from nervous scratching, and from twisting or touching the hair.

For all we hear about "elbows off the table," there are some situations when elbows are not only permitted on the table but actually necessary. This is true in noisy restaurants or clubs, where the only way to hear above the music and chatter is to lean far forward. One is far more graceful leaning forward supported by his or her elbows than doubled forward over hands in the lap. At home, when there is no reason for leaning across the table, there is no reason for elbows. At a formal dinner, elbows may be on the table because, again, one has to lean forward in order to talk to a companion at a distance across the table. But even in these special situations elbows are *never* on the table *when one is eating*.

Tipping one's chair—a most unfortunate habit—is unforgivable. It not only looks sloppy, but is fatal to the back legs of the chair.

When the host fills the plates, he has them passed around the table counterclockwise. Each diner on the right side of the table takes the plate from the person on his left and passes it on to the person on his right. If there is a woman guest on the host's right she keeps the first plate, but the second is passed on to the person at the end of the table. The third goes to the person farthest down on the right side, the next to the person on *his* left, and so on. When all the people on the host's right are served, the plates are sent down the left side, and the host serves himself last. If the hostess is serving, the same order is followed from her end.

Often, "family style" means that the host or hostess serves the meat, but the other dishes are passed around with each diner helping himself. These dishes, too, are passed counterclockwise. Men do not offer the dish to the women on their right first, but help themselves when the dish reaches them. A man may then, if he wishes, hold the dish while the woman next to him serves herself.

At a family meal, plates may be served in the kitchen and brought out to the table. It is better not to do this when guests are present, however. Guests should have the prerogative of serving themselves. Exceptions: individually arranged dishes, such as eggs Benedict, that must be put together in the kitchen.

There should never be any question of which silver to use: *You always start with the implement of each type that is farthest from the plate.* This question arises again and again, and the answer is always the same, with one exception. If the table is incorrectly set, and you realize that you cannot use the implement for the course that its position indicates, you should, of course, choose the next one that is appropriate. Otherwise, you assume that the table is correctly set, and, starting at the outside, work your way with each course toward the center.

Some people are not clear on how to hold flatware. Many just grip the implements with their hands in a fist. It is much more comfortable to hold them lightly. The fork and spoon are held with the thumb and forefinger at a position on the fork that is comfortable, usually about three-quarters of the way up the handle. Your other three fingers then fit loosely and comfortably behind the handle, with the middle finger serving as a support from underneath.

When a fork is used to hold food in place so that it can be cut by a knife, it is held about two-thirds down the handle with the thumb applying pressure from the bottom and the forefinger applying pressure from the top. During this process, the knife is held about halfway down the handle with the thumb and middle finger, while the forefinger presses firmly on the top of the blade where it joins the handle.

Reaching for something across the table—a serving dish, perhaps—is only correct when it does not involve stretching across your neighbor or leaning far across the table yourself. If the item you want is not close at hand, simply ask the person nearest to it, "Would you please pass the butter, George?"

Passing the salt does not necessitate passing the pepper as well. It's OK to do so, but there is no rule that says you have to pass both at once. And speaking of salt, never salt your food without tasting it first—it's insulting to the hostess or chef and could spoil the taste of food that may have been amply seasoned during preparation.

If a condiment or other item is not on the table, it is perfectly correct to ask the hostess for it, if it is obvious that the accompaniment is ordinarily served with the meal and its absence an oversight. Do not, however, ask for anything rare or unusual that your hostess is not likely to have.

People are often confused about how to hold a serving spoon and fork. When lifting food from a serving dish, the spoon is held underneath, with the fork prongs turned down to help hold the portion on the spoon.

When you don't want something that is passed or served to you, simply pass it to the person on your right. You may, if the dish or platter is large, offer to hold it for the next person. If the dish is offered to you by a server, simply say, "No, thank you." You shouldn't, in either case, explain that you are allergic or especially dislike Brussels sprouts, or give any reason for your refusal unless the server or person to your left is inappropriately insistent that you just try a little.

The circumstances determine whether or not it is acceptable to ask for a second helping at a dinner party. It is not acceptable at a formal dinner but is permissible at an informal one. At a formal dinner second helpings are to be offered. A good hostess notices when guests are ready for another portion and asks her server to please pass the meat and rice again. If there are no helpers and the host has served the entrée from a sideboard, he or the hostess will usually urge guests to pass their plates for a second helping. To do this, leave the silver on the plate, making sure it is securely positioned. Never hold your silver in your hand or put it on the tablecloth when you pass your plate. As a courtesy, when only one person takes a second helping a considerate hostess will take a little too—that way, her guest won't feel self-conscious or that he is holding everyone else up.

Help yourself to bread using your fingers. Place the bread, roll, crackers, or whatever on your butter plate. Don't butter the whole piece at once, but instead break off manageable pieces, and butter and eat them one at a time.

Never turn your wineglass or coffee cup upside down to indicate that you want neither. Just say, "No, thank you" to the person pouring, or, if someone does pour wine, coffee, or another beverage into your glass or cup, just quietly leave it there. The fact that you do not drink it indicates that you don't care for any more.

BIG DO'S AND DON'TS OF GRACIOUS DINING

Being at ease at the table—whether for dinner, breakfast, or lunch—means being able to thoroughly enjoy the company and the cuisine. If you spend your minutes at the table being anxious about doing the right thing at the right time, the pleasure that communal meals can bring is dissipated. A review of the following will help make any host or guest at any table comfortable, relaxed, and proficient at gracious dining.

- Do remember to say "please" and "thank you" frequently.
- Do eat quietly. Do not slurp, smack your lips, crunch, or make other noises as you chew or swallow.
- Do always chew with your mouth closed.
- Do chew your food well, putting your utensils down between bites.
- Do wipe your fingers and your mouth frequently with your napkin. Use a corner of the napkin and blot at your mouth; don't wad up the napkin and scrub your face with it.
- Don't encircle your plate with your arm.
- Don't push your plate back when finished, or lean back and announce "I'm through" or "I'm stuffed." Putting your utensils down across your plate will suffice to show you have finished.
- Don't put liquids in your mouth if it is already filled with food—and don't take huge mouthfuls of anything at anytime.
- Don't crook your finger when picking up a cup or glass. It's an affected mannerism.
- Don't leave your spoon in your cup, soup bowl, or stemmed glass.
- Don't cut up your entire meal before you start to eat. Cut only one or two bites at a time.

- Don't leave half the food on your spoon or fork. Learn to put less on and then eat it in one bite.
- Don't wear an excessive amount of lipstick to the table. Not only can it stain napkins, but it also looks unattractive on the rims of cups and glasses or on the silver. It's a good idea to blot your lipstick prior to dining.

NAPKIN NO-NO'S

How you use your napkin says something about your table manners in general. It's easy. Ordinarily, as soon as you are seated at the dinner table, you put your napkin on your lap. At a formal dinner, however, you don't put it into your lap until your hostess puts hers on her lap first. Here are some other napkin do's and don'ts.

- Do not open your napkin with a violent shake. Unfold it as much as necessary with both hands.
- Never tuck a napkin into a collar, belt, or between the buttons of your shirt.
- When using the napkin, avoid wiping your mouth as if with a washcloth. Blotting or patting the lips is much more appropriate.
- When the meal is finished or if you leave the table during the meal, do not refold or crumple up your napkin. Put the napkin on the left side of your place or, if the plates have been removed, in the center. It should be laid on the table in loose folds so that it does not spread itself out. Another option when leaving the table during a meal is to leave your napkin on your chair, so others needn't see it. At a dinner party the hostess lays her napkin on the table as a signal that the meal is over, and the guests then lay their napkins on the table—not before.
- Do not reinsert napkins into napkin rings at the end of a dinner.

WHEN I'M A GUEST AT A DINNER PARTY, WHAT DO I DO WHEN I...

Q. *...need to cough, sneeze, or blow my nose?*

A. You should excuse yourself from the table and go to the rest room to blow your nose. You might find it necessary to first blow your nose (by way of a few gentle puffs), using your handkerchief or tissue immediately following a

Mealtime Manners

sneeze. Do not use your napkin to blow your nose. Before returning to the table, be sure to wash your hands thoroughly after you're through.

Q. *. . . discover bugs, hair, or other nonedibles in the food?*

A. Try to remove the object without calling attention to it and continue eating. If you are truly repulsed, leave the dish untouched rather than embarrass your hostess in a private home. At a restaurant you may—and should—quietly point out the critter to your waiter and ask for a replacement dish. If the alien object has reached your mouth without your previously noticing it, remove it with your fingers as inconspicuously as possible and place it at the edge of your plate.

Q. *. . . get food stuck in a tooth?*

A. It is not permissible to use a toothpick or to use your fingers to pick at your teeth when at the table. If something stuck in your tooth is actually hurting, excuse yourself from the table and go to the bathroom to remove it. Otherwise, wait until the end of the meal and then go take care of it, asking for a toothpick if necessary.

Q. *. . . spill something?*

A. Pick up jelly, a bit of vegetable, or other solid food with the blade of your knife or a clean spoon. If the spill has caused a stain, and you are at someone's house, dab a little water from your glass on it with the corner of your napkin. Apologize to your hostess, who, in turn, should not add to your embarrassment by calling attention to the accident. At an informal dinner without help, offer to get a cloth or sponge to mop up the liquid and help the hostess clean up in any way you can.

Q. *. . . begin choking on meat or bones?*

A. If a sip of water does not help but a good cough will, cover your mouth with your napkin and cough. Remove the morsel with your fingers and put it on the edge of your plate. If you continue to cough, excuse yourself from the table. In the event that you are really choking, you will be unable to speak. Don't hesitate to get someone's attention to help you. The seriousness of your condition will quickly be recognized, and it is no time to worry about manners. Keeping calm and acting quickly might well save your life.

Q. *. . . am faced with a finger bowl?*

A. Finger bowls are generally small glass bowls filled halfway to three-quarters of the way with cold water and are most often seen at formal meals. They are there for the purpose of freshening one's fingers after a meal or after eating a hands-on food such as snails, corn on the cob, or hard-shelled seafood. Finger bowls are placed at the side of each diner's place after a hands-on dinner, or on the dessert plate at a formal dinner.

Dip your fingers, one hand at a time, into the water and then dry your fingers on your napkin. If a finger bowl is brought directly before dessert, it is often placed on a doily on the dessert plate. To remove it, lift it, with the doily underneath, and move it to the upper left of your place setting.

A slice of lemon is never used in a finger bowl at a formal dinner, but flowers may be floated in it. Lemon may be floated in a finger bowl used after an informal dinner of lobster.

In some restaurants, moist steamed hand towels are brought to the table at the conclusion of the meal. These are held in tongs and presented to the diner. Take the towel, use it to wipe your hands and, if necessary, around your mouth. Diligent waiters will hover and take the towel from you the minute you are finished. If your waiter disap-
pears, just put the towel at the side of
your place on the table.

Q. *. . . have to use a saltcellar?*

A. Some hostesses prefer to use old-
fashioned saltcellars, which salt shakers
have largely replaced. If there is no
spoon in the saltcellar, use the tip of a
clean knife to take some salt. If the saltcellar is for you alone, you may either
use the tip of your knife or you may
take a pinch with your fingers. If it is to be shared with others, never use your fingers or a knife that is not clean. Salt you have dipped into should be put on the bread-and-butter plate or on the rim of whatever plate is before you.

Q. *. . . eat food that is too hot or food that tastes spoiled?*

A. If a bite of food is too hot, quickly take a swallow of water. If there is no cold beverage at all, and your mouth is scalding, you can spit the food out, preferably onto your fork or into your fingers, and from there place it quickly on the edge of the plate. The same is true of spoiled food. Should you eat a bad oyster or clam, for example, don't swallow it. Remove it as quickly and unobtru-
sively as you can. To spit anything whatsoever into the corner of your napkin is not permissible.

HOW TO EAT CERTAIN FOODS

The basic etiquette of eating all foods is that they be transported to the mouth in manageable, bite-size pieces. Certain courses and foods, however, require special dexterity. One of the greatest tests a gracious diner faces is to be presented with a food he is unfamiliar with. Yet even familiar foods can be challenging when dining in a formal setting, where some dishes aren't meant to be eaten as casually as you might eat them at home.

When presented with a food you have never eaten before, such as escargots, what you do depends on the company you are in. If among friends, there is nothing embarrassing about saying, "I've never had escargots before. Please show me how to do this." If you're at a formal function or among strangers, however, you may not want to admit to this. In this case, it is best to delay beginning by having a sip of water or wine and watching what others are doing.

Certain foods, such as chicken drumsticks, are generally eaten in informal settings with the fingers, and in many homes, asparagus is a finger food. But what happens when a diner at a formal table is faced with asparagus drenched in Hollandaise sauce? Does he pluck a spear with his fingers, throw his head back, and toss the sauce-laden vegetable into his mouth, dripping Hollandaise down his pleated shirt? Or does he follow the lead of other diners and cut his spears neatly with knife and fork? (The correct answer: the latter.) The primary advice on how to eat particular foods, then, is to take into consideration the properties of the foods, how they are served, and to gauge the environment before proceeding.

APPLES AND PEARS

Slice into quarters, core each quarter, and cut into slices, which are then eaten with the fingers.

APRICOTS

See under **Cherries, Apricots, and Plums.**

ARTICHOKES

Whole artichokes are always eaten with the fingers. Begin at the outside base of the artichoke and pull off one leaf at a time. Dip the base of the leaf, which is the softer meaty end of it, into melted butter, if provided, and then place it between your teeth and pull it forward. The leaves closer to the center will have a greater edible portion than those at the outside. Place the inedible portion of each leaf neatly on the side of your plate.

When the leaves are all consumed and you reach the center of the artichoke, scrape away the thistle-like part with your knife. This fuzzy portion is inedible and is called the choke. Place this along the side of your plate with the leaves. The remaining part of the artichoke is the heart, or bottom. Cut this into bite-size pieces with a knife and fork and dip the pieces into the melted butter before eating.

ASPARAGUS

Although asparagus is by reputation a finger food, you should always use utensils to eat it at all but the most informal dining situations. In the case of the latter, you may pick asparagus up with your fingers when it is prepared al dente and the stalks are firm, and any sauce is only on the tips. Eat it one stalk at a time, from the tip to the opposite end in manageable bites. When the stalks are covered in sauce or are limp, then cut them with your fork or fork and knife and eat them in small pieces. All hard ends should be cut off asparagus before it is served. If this has not been done, do not attempt to eat the ends: If you can't cut them, you can't chew them.

AVOCADOS

When avocado slices are served, cut and eat with a fork. When avocados are served in halves, hold the shell to steady it with one hand and eat the fruit with a spoon. Leave the empty shell, which is inedible, on the plate. When a salad or other mixture is served in an avocado shell, it is permissible to hold the shell lightly with one hand while eating the contents with a fork held in the other hand.

BACON

Eat breakfast bacon with a fork if limp; if it is dry and crisp, use your fingers.

BANANAS

Peel halfway down and eat bite by bite at the family table, but when dining out it is better to peel the skin all the way off, lay the fruit on your plate, cut it in slices, and eat it with a fork.

BEVERAGES, HOT

When served in a cup with a saucer, place the spoon at the side of the saucer, as you do a tea bag. If the beverage slops onto a saucer, and no replacement is available, it is fine to pour the liquid back into the cup and use a paper napkin to dry the bottom of the cup. When your hot beverage is served in a mug, never leave the spoon in the mug. If the tablecloth or mats are fabric, rest the bowl of the spoon face down on the edge of a butter or dinner plate, with the handle on the table. If the tablecloth is paper or plastic, you may lick the spoon clean and lay it beside the mug. Beverages that are too hot to drink may be sipped, never slurped, from a spoon.

BREAD AND BUTTER

Break the bread with your fingers into moderate-size pieces. To butter it, hold a piece on the edge of the bread-and-butter plate and spread enough butter on it for a mouthful or two at a time. If there is no butter knife, use any other knife that is available.

BREAD, ROUND LOAF ON CUTTING BOARD

Some restaurants present an entire round loaf of bread on a cutting board for you to slice yourself. This should be cut not like a round cake in wedges, but in slices. Starting at one side, thinly slice the crust off, and then slice toward the center.

BREAKFAST PASTRIES

Cut Danish pastry or sticky buns in half or in quarters with a knife and eat with the fingers, if not too sticky, or with a fork. Cut muffins in half either vertically or horizontally, and butter one half at a time. Open and butter croissants or popovers, and then eat in small pieces with your fingers.

BUTTER

Butter bread, biscuits, toast, pancakes, and corn on the cob with a knife. For corn that has been cut off the cob, rice, or potatoes, mix butter in with a fork.

When pats of butter are served, lift them with the utensil provided (most often a butter knife or small fork) and transfer them to your own plate. When butter is served as a block, cut a pat from one end and transfer it to your bread-and-butter plate or dinner plate. If there is no accompanying utensil, transfer the butter with your own clean knife. When butter is presented in a tub, scoop a portion with your own knife or butter knife and place it on your bread-and-butter plate or dinner plate.

In a restaurant, when butter is offered in individually wrapped squares, open the wrapper and use your knife to push the square onto your plate, folding the buttery side of the wrapper in and placing it on the edge of the plate, never on the tablecloth.

CANTALOUPES AND MELONS

Served in halves or wedges, melons should be eaten with a spoon. When served in precut pieces, eat with a fork.

CAVIAR

Use the spoon with which it is presented to place the caviar on your plate. Using your own knife or spoon, then place small amounts on toast triangles, which may be buttered or not. If chopped egg, minced onions, or sour cream are served with caviar, one or more of these toppings is spooned, sparingly, on top of the caviar.

CHERRIES, APRICOTS, AND PLUMS

Eat with the fingers. The pit of the fruit should be made as clean as possible in your mouth and then dropped into your almost closed, cupped hand and then to your plate. Plums and apricots are held in your fingers and eaten as close to the pit as possible. When you remove a pit with your fingers, do so with your thumb underneath and your first two fingers across your mouth, not with your fingertips pointing into your mouth. Or push the pit forward with the tongue onto a spoon and then drop it onto a plate.

CHERRY TOMATOES

Except when served in a salad or other dish, cherry tomatoes are eaten with the fingers. And they squirt! The best thing to do is to try to select one small enough to be put in your mouth whole. Even then, close your lips tightly before chewing. If you must bite into a larger one, make a little break in the skin with your front teeth before biting it in half. When served whole in a salad or other dish, cherry tomatoes are cut, carefully, with a knife and fork and eaten with the fork.

CHICKEN, TURKEY, AND OTHER FOWL

At a formal dinner, no part of a bird is picked up with the fingers. However, among family and friends and in family-style or informal restaurants, it is permissible to do so—particularly if it is fried.

The main body of the bird, however, is not eaten with the fingers. Cut off as much meat as you can from the main body and leave the rest on your plate. To eat the small bones, such as the joint or wing, hold the piece of bone with meat on it up to your mouth and eat it clean. Larger joints, too, such as the drumstick of a roast chicken, may be picked up after the first few easily cut pieces have been eaten.

CHOPS

At a dinner party or in a formal restaurant lamb chops must be eaten with knife and fork. Cut the center, or eye, of the chop off the bone into two or three pieces. At the family table or in an informal group of friends, the center may be cut out and eaten with the fork, and the bone picked up and eaten clean with the teeth. This is permissible, too, with veal or pork chops, but only when they are broiled or otherwise served without sauce. When picking up a chop with your fingers, hold it with one hand only. If it is too big to hold with only one hand, it is too big to pick up.

CLAMS, MUSSELS, AND OYSTERS

Clams and oysters on the half shell are generally served on cracked ice and arranged around a container of cocktail sauce. Hold the shell with the fingers of your left hand and the shellfish fork (or smallest fork provided) with the right hand. Spear the clam or oyster with the fork, dip it into sauce, and eat it in one bite. If a part of the clam or oyster sticks to the shell, use your fork to separate it from the shell. Or take a little of the sauce on your fork and drop it onto the clam or squeeze a little lemon onto it before eating.

When raw clams or oysters are ordered at a clam bar or eaten at a picnic, you may pick up the shell with the fingers and suck the clam or oyster and its juice right off the shell.

Steamed clams should be open at least halfway. If they aren't, don't eat them. Open the shell fully, holding it with your left hand, and pull out the clam with your fingers if the setting is informal, or with a seafood fork if it is more formal. If the clam is a true steamer, slip the skin off the neck with your fingers and put it aside. Dip steamed clams into broth and/or melted butter and eat in one bite. Empty shells are placed in a bowl provided for that purpose, or around the edge of your plate if there is no bowl.

Mussels, like some steamed clams, may be served in their shells in the broth in which they are steamed. The mussel may be removed from its shell with a fork, then dipped into the sauce and eaten in one bite. It is permissible to pick up the shell, scooping a little of the juice with it, and suck the mussel and juice directly off the shell. The juice or broth remaining in the bowl may be eaten with a spoon, or you may sop it up with pieces of a roll or French bread speared on the tines of your fork.

CORN ON THE COB

Whether using your fingers or the little ear-holders, eat corn on the cob as neatly and gently as possible. If melted butter has not been added in the kitchen, take pats of butter from the butter plate and place them on your dinner plate. Butter and season only a few rows of the corn at a time, repeating this process until the corn is finished.

FETTUCCINE

See under **Spaghetti, Linguini, and Fettuccine.**

FISH

Fish served in fillet form is eaten with a fork and knife. If you find small bones in your mouth when eating fish, push them to the front of your mouth with your tongue and then onto your fork, removing them to the side of the plate.

FOWL

See under **Chicken, Turkey, and Other Fowl.**

FRENCH FRIES

When French-fried potatoes accompany finger foods, such as hamburgers, hot dogs, or other sandwiches, they may be eaten with the fingers—unless they are covered with sauce, such as ketchup. At other times they should be cut into reasonable lengths and eaten with a fork.

GRAPES

Avoid pulling grapes off the bunch one at a time. Instead, choose a branch with several grapes on it and break it off or cut off with scissors. Seedless grapes are no problem to eat at all, since the entire fruit, skin and all, is eaten. Grapes with seeds, however, are more of a challenge and can be eaten one of two ways. First, you may lay the grape on its side, holding it with the fingers of one hand, and cut in the center with the point of a knife, which also lifts and removes the seeds. Or pop the grape in your mouth whole and then deposit the seeds into your fingers and place them on your plate as elegantly as possible. Concord or garden grapes with difficult-to-digest skin should be pressed between your lips and against your almost-closed teeth so that the juice and pulp will be drawn into your mouth and the skin left to be discarded.

GRAVIES AND SAUCES

You may sop bread into gravy, but it must be done by putting a small piece down on the gravy and then eating it with your fork as though it were any other helping on your plate. If it's easier for you, you may put it into your mouth "continental" style, with the tines pointed down as they were when you sopped up the gravy. A good sauce may also be finished in this way.

ICED TEA OR COFFEE

If it is served on a saucer, rest the spoon on that. If not, rest the spoon as you would a spoon served with a mug, described on p.184 under Beverages, Hot.

KIWI

Peel this fuzzy-skinned fruit and slice like a tomato. If presented with an unpeeled kiwi, use a sharp paring knife to peel away the outer skin, which is inedible, and slice the kiwi crosswise, further cutting it into bite-size pieces and eating it with a fork. The seeds are edible.

LASAGNA

See under Ziti, Lasagna, and Layered Pasta.

LINGUINI

See under Spaghetti, Linguini, and Fettuccine.

LOBSTER

It's a good idea to crack lobster shells at all points before you serve them. Provide each guest with individual nutcrackers or shellfish crackers to finish the process—as well as with seafood forks for extracting the lobster meat. Place a large bowl or platter for discarded empty shells on the table and give a big paper napkin or plastic bib to each lobster eater.

Crack claws slowly so that the juice does not squirt when the shell breaks. Holding the lobster steady with one hand and the nutcracker in your other hand, twist off the claws from the body and place them on the side of your plate. Crack each claw and pull out the meat. The meat is removed from the large

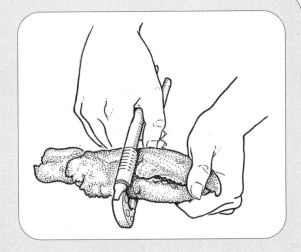

claw ends and from each joint with a shellfish fork or a knife. The tail meat is pulled out of the shell in two solid pieces—one side at a time. Cut into bite-size pieces and dip into melted butter, if hot, or mayonnaise, if cold. The red roe and the green "fat" or "tamale" are edible and delectable to some, who like to combine them with the lobster meat. Real lobster lovers get an additional morsel out of the legs by breaking off one at a time, putting them into the mouth and biting up the shell, squeezing the meat out of the broken end.

The host should have finger bowls with warm water and lemon slices at the side of each place as soon as people are finished eating. These are carried away after the dinner plates have been removed.

MEATS, BARBECUED

Because the nature of a barbecue is informal, eating barbecued foods should be informal. When ribs, chicken pieces, hamburgers, and hot dogs are served, use your fingers. Eat steak, fish, and other meats served in larger portions with a fork.

MELONS

See under **Cantaloupes and Melons.**

MUSSELS

See under **Clams, Mussels, and Oysters.**

OLIVES

Eat olives with your fingers when they are served as a relish. If there are stones, bite off the meat of the olive but don't actually "clean" the stone. Remove the stone from your mouth with your fingers, or by pushing it with your tongue onto a spoon. Bite a large stuffed olive in half. Put only a very small one in your mouth whole. When the olive is in a salad, eat it with your fork, not your fingers.

ORANGES AND TANGERINES

Eat these citrus fruits by slicing the two ends of the rind off first and then cutting the peel off in vertical strips. If the peel is thick and loose, it can be pulled off with the fingers. Tangerines are easily broken apart into small sections by hand, while oranges may need to be cut with a knife. Seeds should be taken out from the center with the tip of the knife and sections eaten with the fingers. If there is fiber around the peeled orange or tangerine, it may be removed with the fingers. Any remaining fiber and seeds can be removed from the mouth neatly with the thumb and first two fingers (fingers above and thumb underneath).

OYSTERS

See under **Clams, Mussels, and Oysters.**

PASTA, LAYERED

See under **Ziti, Lasagna, and Layered Pasta.**

PASTRIES

See under **Breakfast Pastries.**

PEAS

Peas are perhaps one of the most difficult foods to capture and eat. You may use your knife as a pusher to get them onto your fork, or you may use the tines of the fork to actually spear a few peas at a time.

PEACHES

Peel and then eat with knife and fork.

PEARS

See under **Apples and Pears.**

PIE

Eat with a fork; if à la mode, you may use a spoon.

PINEAPPLE

This prickly tropical fruit is sliced into round pieces and served on a plate to be eaten with a dessert fork and spoon.

PIZZA

Pizza is cut into wedges with a knife or pizza cutter and served this way. Individual wedges may be picked up and eaten with the fingers. Some pizza lovers prefer to fold the pizza vertically at the center to keep edges from hanging outward and dripping before lifting it to their mouths. Pizza may also be cut into bite-size pieces with a knife and fork and eaten with a fork.

PLUMS

See under Cherries, Apricots, and Plums.

SALAD

If your salad has large leaves of lettuce, it is perfectly fine to cut the lettuce with a knife and fork into small pieces. Cut only one or two bites at a time. Never attack your entire salad, cutting the entire plateful into small pieces at once.

SANDWICHES

All ordinary sandwiches are eaten with the fingers. Club sandwiches and other sandwiches an inch thick or more are best cut into small portions before being picked up and held tightly in the fingers of both hands. Naturally, sandwiches that are served with gravy, such as hot turkey or roast beef sandwiches, are cut with a knife and fork and eaten with a fork.

SASHIMI

See under Sushi and Sashimi.

SAUCES

See under Gravies and Sauces.

SHISH KEBAB

Except for shish kebab served as an hors d'oeuvre, you do not eat directly from the skewer. When shish kebab is served as a main course, lift the skewer with one hand and with the other, use your fork, beginning with the pieces at the bottom, to push and slide the meat and vegetables off the skewer and onto your plate. Place the emptied skewer on the edge of your plate, and with your knife and fork, cut the meat and vegetables into manageable pieces a bite at a time.

SHRIMP COCKTAIL

If not too large, each shrimp should be eaten in one bite. When shrimp are of jumbo size, the diner has no alternative but to grasp the cup in which they are served firmly with one hand and cut the shrimp as neatly as possible with the edge of the fork. It is impractical to use a knife because the stemmed shrimp cup will tip over unless held with one hand. If the saucer or plate under the shrimp cup is large enough, you might remove a shrimp from the cup, place it on the saucer, and cut it there with a knife and fork. The problem can be avoided by arranging shrimp attractively on a small plate—where they can easily be cut with knife or fork. When shrimp are served as an hors d'oeuvre, pick them up by their tails, dip them (once) into the sauce, and then discard the tail into the receptacle provided.

Eat shrimp cocktail with the smallest fork at your place. If a lemon wedge is served with the shrimp, spear it with your fork and, covering the back of the wedge with your other hand, squeeze it carefully over the shrimp. If individual sauce bowls are offered, dip your shrimp into the sauce. If the sauce dish is shared, spoon it from the dish over the shrimp.

SNAILS (ESCARGOTS)

Grasp snail shells with a special holder or with the fingers of one hand if no holder is provided. With the other hand, remove 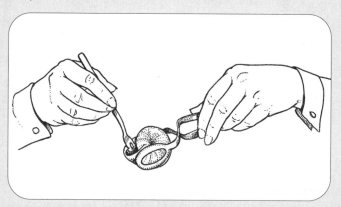 the meat with a small fork. Pour any garlic butter that remains in the shells onto the snail plate and sop up with small pieces of French bread on the end of a fork.

SOUP

If the soup is served in a cup with handles, you may drink from the cup or just use a spoon. When served in a shallow soup plate and the level of soup is so low that you must tip the plate to avoid scraping the bottom, lift the near edge and tip the plate away from you, never toward you. Spoon the soup either away from you or toward you, whichever is less awkward. Soups such as French onion, which is served with a crouton in the bowl and cheese baked and bubbled on the top, require two utensils for eating. The soup spoon is used to eat the soup, while a knife or even a fork is required to cut the cheese on the rim of the soup cup or dish so that it does not trail from bowl to mouth in a long string. Initially, when the bowl is full and there is danger of splashing, it is not incorrect to take a small amount of the cheese on the spoon and twist it around the bowl of the spoon, cutting it neatly at the edge with the fork or knife. The spoon may then be dipped into the bowl so that a spoonful of soup is eaten with the cheese already on the spoon.

SPAGHETTI, LINGUINI, AND FETTUCCINE

There are three ways to eat stringy pasta—none difficult to master. The first is to take a few strands on your fork and twirl the spaghetti around the fork, holding the tines against the edge of your plate. The second is to hold the fork in one hand and a large, dessert-size spoon in the other. Take a few strands of the pasta on the fork and place the tines against the bowl of the spoon, twirling the fork to wrap the spaghetti around itself as it turns. The third is simply to cut spaghetti (linguini, fettuccine, or other long pasta) into sections and eat it with a fork.

If the first two methods are used, the spaghetti should be twirled until there are no dangling ends. Bring the fork to your mouth. If ends do unwind themselves from around the fork, you must either suck them (quietly, please!) into your mouth, or bite them neatly, hoping they fall back onto your fork and do not drop to your chest or plate.

When pasta is served with the sauce ladled on top and not mixed in, mix it neatly, using a fork and spoon, before eating.

SUSHI AND SASHIMI

Sushi is served in small pieces that may be eaten whole. If you're using a fork and the pieces are too large, you may cut them with the fork or with a fork and sharp knife. If eaten with chopsticks, the fish is picked up whole and eaten from the chopsticks, or the ends of the chopsticks may be used to cut the portions into smaller pieces. If you're using your fingers and the piece is large, you may bite it in half. When soy sauce is provided, one end of the sushi portions may be dipped into it and put in the mouth. Sashimi, which is thinly sliced boneless fish, is generally eaten with chopsticks. If you are serving yourself from a serving platter of sushi or sashimi, you should turn your chopsticks around and pick up pieces with the large end, which has not touched your mouth.

TACOS AND TORTILLAS

Eat tacos and tortillas with the hands—it is impossible to cut into the crisp shell with a knife and fork without having it crack and crumble. Eat any filling that falls out, however with a fork, not with your hands.

TANGERINES

See under **Oranges and Tangerines.**

TORTILLAS

See under **Tacos and Tortillas.**

TURKEY

See under **Chicken, Turkey, and Other Fowl.**

ZITI, LASAGNA, AND LAYERED PASTA

Melted, stringy mozzarella cheese from layered pasta dishes can stubbornly stretch from the dish to your mouth and be difficult to cut off. Before you take a bite, slice portions and cut through the cheese. This prevents the rather unattractive sight of strings of cheese hanging from your mouth and chin as you dine.

COCKTAIL AND HORS D'OEUVRES SAVVY

When you are served a beverage with a spoon or swizzle stick (stirrer) in it, you must remove it from the glass before drinking. Do not drink with anything, whether a paper umbrella or a teaspoon, still in the cup or glass in which it is served. At a cocktail party, you must hold the stirrer in your hand until you find a waste receptacle. If, however, the stirrer is actually a straw and you wish to drink through it, it is fine to keep it in the glass. At a restaurant, when there is no plate on which to put a spoon or stirrer, you should let it drip as dry as possible and place it on the table or in an ashtray if no one at the table smokes. At someone's home, you would put a spoon on the saucer, on a plate, or on a paper napkin, never on the tablecloth or on a cloth napkin. It is also acceptable, if there is absolutely nowhere to dispose of a spoon, to ask where you should put it or, if in the home of a good friend or relative, to excuse yourself for a moment and carry it to the kitchen.

When hors d'oeuvres are hot, it's wise to wait a few moments until they cool before putting them in your mouth. Since they are best served bite-size, they can do serious damage to the inside of your mouth if popped in, burning hot, whole. If the appetizer you put in your mouth does not agree with your taste buds, you must push it with your tongue into a cocktail napkin held in your hand, which you then dispose of in a waste receptacle.

If toothpicks are offered, spear the hors d'oeuvre, put it in your mouth, and then place the used toothpick on a plate or receptacle put out for that purpose; you can also hold it in your napkin until you find a wastebasket. Never put a used toothpick back on the serving tray. Do not discard toothpicks, napkins, uneaten appetizers, or remnants in ashtrays, a potentially hazardous practice should a lighted cigarette be placed there.

When appetizers have their own remnants, such as tiny crab claws or shrimp tails, hold them in a paper napkin until such time as you can dispose of them.

When fresh vegetables and dip are offered, dip the vegetable only once, never a second time, after taking a bite of the vegetable. If fresh vegetables are passed as a relish at the table, place them on your bread-and-butter plate or, if there isn't one, on your salad plate or on the edge of whatever plate is in front of you. Never transfer a relish or olive directly from the serving plate to your mouth.

If you want to eat the olives, cherries, or onions served in cocktails, by all means do so. If they are served on a toothpick or cocktail pick, simply remove them from the drink and enjoy them. If there is no pick, drink enough of the cocktail so that you will not wet your fingers, and lift out the olive or cherry and eat it with your fingers. Slices of oranges in old-fashioneds are not usually eaten, as it is too messy to chew the pulp off the rind.

DINING, ORIENTAL STYLE

Those familiar and comfortable with chopsticks should use them when they are offered. Food is usually served in small pieces so that it does not need to be cut. When larger pieces are served, however, the chopsticks, held together, are used to chop or cut the piece in half or to bite-size when possible. Large pieces of meat can be picked up with the chopsticks and eaten by biting off small mouthfuls one at a time.

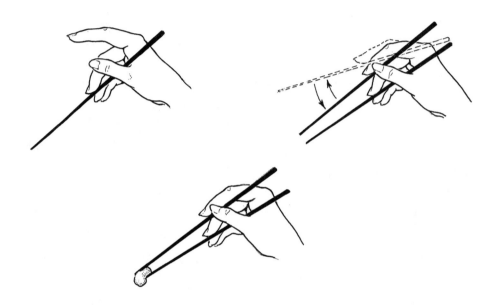

If individual dipping sauces are provided, food is dipped into the dish—the sauce is not poured over the food, as gravy would be ladled onto mashed potatoes. Each bite is held with the chopsticks, dipped, and raised to the mouth.

Rice is almost impossible to grasp in mouthfuls and raise from plate to mouth. Because of this, the individual rice bowl is raised to a point just under the chin, and the chopsticks are used to scoop the rice into the mouth. If a fork is used, then the rice bowl is left on the table and a forkful at a time is brought to the mouth.

Dumplings and other small, stuffed items at restaurants offering dim sum (Chinese appetizers, or little bites) are taken whole with the chopsticks and raised to the mouth. If they are slightly too big to put entirely in the mouth, they may be bitten in half. This can be tricky for the uninitiated, since a firm grasp must be kept on the part that is not being eaten.

Soup is eaten with the flat spoon provided. Even though served in a cup, it usually is not drunk from the cup.

Chinese tea, which is provided by the pot, is poured by whomever is closest to it, with each diner passing his or her cup to the one pouring. A milk or cream pitcher is rarely ever set on a table in an Oriental restaurant—the expectation is that you add nothing but perhaps sugar to your tea. If you must have milk, however, you certainly may ask your waiter to bring it to you. In Japanese restaurants a green tea is often served. This mild tea is not accompanied by sugar or milk.

When large platters are placed on the table, a serving spoon is usually provided to accompany each; diners then serve themselves from the platters, leaving the serving spoon on the platter. If no spoon is provided, chopsticks may be used to transfer food from plate to platter, but they must be turned around so that the larger end, the one that has not been in the mouth, is used.

RESTAURANT TABLE MANNERS

Do restaurant table manners differ from the manners one uses at home? Although table manners are much the same whether you are eating at home or at a restaurant, a few special situations arise when dining out.

- When vegetables and potatoes are served in individual side dishes, you may eat them directly from small dishes or put them on your dinner plate by using a serving spoon or sliding them directly out of the small dish. Ask the waiter to remove any empty dishes, to avoid an overcrowded table.
- When an uncut loaf of bread is placed on the table, the host—or the diner closest to the bread—slices or breaks off two or three individual portions and offers them with the rest of the loaf in the breadbasket or on the plate to the people beside him. This is then passed around the table for diners to cut the bread for themselves and possibly their neighbors.
- If coffee or tea is placed on the table without first having been poured by the waiter, the person nearest the pot should offer to pour, filling his or her own cup last.
- If sugar, crackers, cream, or other accompaniments to meals are served with paper wrappers or in plastic or cardboard containers, the wrappers should be

crumpled up tightly and either tucked under the rim of your plate or placed on the edge of the saucer or butter plate. Don't put them in the ashtray if smokers are present, since their lighted cigarettes could easily set the paper on fire.

- Don't wipe off tableware in a restaurant. If your silverware is dirty, simply ask the waiter or waitress for a clean one. If you spill wine or water in a restaurant, try quietly to attract the attention of the waiter.
- When you are dining at a restaurant buffet, never go back to the buffet for a refill with a dirty plate. Leave it for the waitperson to pick up and start afresh with a clean plate.
- Tasting another person's food at the table is permissible if done unobtrusively. Never reach over and spear something off someone else's plate, however, or feed someone across the table. Either hand your fork to your dinner partner, have them spear a bite and then hand it back to you, or have them place a portion on your plate.
- At the end of a meal a woman may quickly put on a little lipstick, but to look in a mirror and daub at the face is in bad taste.
- The one never-to-be-broken rule is: Never use a comb at a restaurant table— or in any public place. Never rearrange or put your hands to your hair in any place where food is served. These rules apply to both men and women.

TABLE MANNERS FOR KIDS

Teaching table manners to children is a building-block process. Generally, table manners for children are the same as they are for adults, but should be geared to the child's age. It is a very different thing to tell a child in a high chair to "act your age" than it is to say the same to a five-year-old.

Practice makes perfect: Young children need to be reminded, gently and repeatedly, of the courtesies that adults take for granted. And set a good example! Teach them the following:

- BE NEAT AND CLEAN Make hand washing a habit. Teach your child to wash his hands and face before he comes to a table to eat. Instead of ordering children to do this, tell them why. Explain about germs and how pleasant it is to eat and talk with someone who made herself look nice, out of respect for everyone else. When children understand the reason for doing something, it is easier for them to remember to do it.

- **EAT IN SMALL BITES**   First, because it isn't safe to have more in your mouth than you can manage, and second, because it is unattractive to sit with anyone who can't close his lips or who has bits of food spewing from his mouth. Thus, chew with the mouth closed.

- **DO NOT FLOAT FOOD DOWN YOUR THROAT WITH DRINKS**   Again, there is a safety factor at work, but there is also a politeness factor, since a child has to open a mouthful of food in order to swallow a beverage. A rule could be that the mouth opens to receive a spoonful or forkful of food, and it doesn't open again until that food is chewed, with the mouth closed, and swallowed.

- **FOOD NOISES ARE UNACCEPTABLE**   Lips are not smacked; drinks are not gulped.

- **NAPKINS, NOT SLEEVES OR HANDS, ARE FOR WIPING MOUTHS**   They are meant to be used regularly throughout the meal. Why? Because it is hard for anyone to know if he has a milk mustache or ketchup on his cheek. Using the napkin periodically takes care of what otherwise might be an embarrassing sight.

- **THERE IS A CORRECT WAY TO HOLD AND USE UTENSILS**   Start out with younger children using a spoon. By age five or six most children can learn to be adept at using a fork and knife. By age six, children should learn how to cut food and how to properly hold a fork and spoon: not in a fist, but comfortably with the thumb and forefinger, about three-quarters of the way down the handle.

- **LEARN TO MAKE PLEASANT MEALTIME CONVERSATION**   Do not criticize the food and do thank the hostess or cook upon finishing the meal.

- **ASK TO BE EXCUSED FROM THE TABLE**   Children should be permitted to be excused from the table, when very young, if the meal is an extended one. Expecting a young child to sit quietly through a protracted meal when his food is gone is an unreasonable demand on his patience and ability to sit still without wiggling, fiddling, and noisemaking to help pass the time. "May I please be excused?" should be asked of parents or of the hostess when dining with friends and relatives.

THE PROBLEM SANDWICH

Q. *I attended a lunch the other day and was served beautiful open-faced sandwiches on English muffins. I was at a loss, however, on the best way to eat them. Should I have cut up the sandwich and eaten the bites with a fork or could I have picked it up with my fingers and taken a bite?*

A. It depends on several factors. One, if the open-faced sandwich is small and fairly self-contained, so that it doesn't fall to pieces when you pick it up with fingers, you may do so. Second, if the sandwich is large and unwieldy or slathered in gravy or sauce, common sense tells you to cut it up and eat it with a fork. And third, the way you eat an open-faced sandwich depends on the occasion. If you are attending a formal dinner, by all means eat the sandwich with a knife and fork.

CHAPTER 24

ACCIDENTS, MISHAPS, AND BOORISH BEHAVIOR

Emily Post prided herself on remaining cool and unflappable when confronted with embarrassing mishaps. When she fell down some stairs and broke her foot, she kept calm—and her hat stayed on straight during the entire fall. My great-grandmother-in-law understood that we are, after all, "human beings and not robots." Accidents and mishaps will happen, but they don't have to mar a good time. Boorish behavior, too, can be deflected with grace and ease by the smart host or hostess.

ACCIDENTS AND MISHAPS

There may be nothing more gracious than the host who thoughtfully reassures a guest who accidentally spills or breaks something. Making a guest feel worse than he already does accomplishes nothing. The host who quickly smoothes over the incident or makes a joke out of it is truly a considerate one. The same goes for the other guests. If you are a guest and another guest makes a mistake or damages an item, the rudest thing you can do is to point it out; so don't.

When a guest accidentally breaks a plate or a glass, however, it is up to him to offer to pay to replace it. While the guest's manners are obviously lacking if he doesn't at least offer, it is never correct for the host to remind him of his responsibility—even if what was lost was expensive or irreplaceable. Accidents do happen, and breakage is the cost of entertaining when guests are inconsiderate.

If, on the other hand, a guest breaks something and insists on paying for it, but you feel uncomfortable billing him for the replacement, do and say nothing. If he persists, then you are perfectly correct in giving him an estimate on the cost.

If you are a guest at a party and accidentally break something, try to get an estimate of the item from your host. If he refuses, send him a check with a note that reads something like: "I feel terrible about breaking your dish and would like to make full restitution. I have enclosed a check that I hope covers the loss, but if it doesn't, please let me know." Or, you can try to find a replacement just like the one that was broken, especially if it is part of a set.

Some homeowners' insurance policies cover breakage in another's home. It is wise to check your policy before you buy a replacement; you just might be reimbursed.

INEBRIATED GUESTS

When someone has had too much to drink and becomes obnoxious or embarrassing at your party, it can be embarrassing for all concerned. First, enlist the aid of the person or people he came with in getting the overindulger home or in helping should he be feeling sick. If the drunken person has come to the party alone, ask a friend to help you assist him or her to a bedroom or a taxi. If the reveler is merely on the way to becoming loud, try to keep him from having any more to drink—to the point of saying you think perhaps he or she has had enough or by asking, "How about a cup of coffee?" When a drunk becomes insulting or offensive, as sometimes happens, be sure to smooth it over with the person he has insulted, explaining that "Jim [or Joanne] has had a little too much to drink, and really doesn't know what he [or she] is saying." Then get Jim or Joanne diverted and away from the bar.

Most important, never let anyone who has had too much to drink get behind the wheel of a car. If there is no one to do the driving, either see that a mutual friend takes him home safely, call a taxi, or put him to bed in your home. Your guest's car keys should be taken away if he refuses to go with someone else. This is for the safety of other travelers as well as your guest. Another important issue is the growing trend of finding a host or hostess legally liable if injury comes to the drinker or someone else. For all of these reasons, you must prevent an inebriated guest from driving.

If, on the other hand, *you* are the overimbibing offender who disrupted the party, you must recognize that your behavior was insulting or rude—and you should apologize immediately. If you felt yourself getting drunk, however, and left the party without embarrassing yourself, the other guests, or your hosts, you'll have nothing to apologize for except perhaps an early departure.

You can mention this when you make your thank-you call by saying, "Your party was terrific! I'm sorry I left a little early, but I had too much to drink and thought it was best to go before I passed out on your couch."

ETHNIC SLURS AND OFFENSIVE JOKES

If you find yourself in a social situation with people who make their prejudices known with ethnic slurs, you can do one of a number of things. If you find another's opinion totally unacceptable, try to change the subject as soon as possible. If that doesn't work, excuse yourself from the conversation, particularly if you care intensely about the subject and might become emotional in your response.

If you belong to the group under attack, you have two choices. You can simply ignore it and avoid those people in the future. Or, you can bluntly say: "You must be talking about me. I'm Irish [or whatever it is]." Their shocked embarrassment can be almost as rewarding as their limp efforts to make amends; one can only hope this will temper their prejudice in the future. If there are people of the targeted group with you or in hearing range, your situation is more embarrassing. Try to change the conversation if you can. If you cannot, avoid the urge to rise to the defense, which might evoke an onslaught even more embarrassing to your friends. Keep your silence, break away when possible, and apologize profusely to them in private.

If you find yourself in a social gathering with a person who makes offensive jokes, you should feel no need to laugh or support such a display of poor taste. If you are the host, you need only interrupt him in the middle of the joke to ask for his help in another room. You can take him aside and tell him you think he has a wonderful sense of humor but that he may be embarrassing the other guests by telling off-color jokes. If you are a guest who is offended by what another guest is saying, you may quietly say, "I don't appreciate that kind of remark," or "I dislike jokes that put others down." If the offensive slurs continue, turn your back or simply take your leave.

DROP-INS AND UNEXPECTED VISITS

Visits to friends, acquaintances, and even relative strangers range from spontaneous, informal drop-in visits to formal calls, with their own protocol and etiquette. The only etiquette involved in casual visits between close friends is that they be considerate of each other and that they never abuse the special bond of their friendship.

It is a poor idea in general to drop in on someone unexpectedly. Yet there is always the occasional relative, friend, or neighbor who thinks nothing of walking right in without knocking. If it bothers you, I say: lock your doors. While an occasional unannounced drop-in works out well—especially if it is immediate family or a close friend—more often it is inconvenient to the one visited. The host may have previous plans, may not be feeling well, may be in the middle of something, or may simply be resting or relaxing. The sight of an eager visitor at the door, primed for an hour or two of conversation, is rarely an undiluted pleasure.

It is not a good idea, therefore, to visit without calling beforehand. Agree to a time that is convenient for both of you. You may do so with a telephone call or, if you live some distance away, in a note. In the latter case it should be written far enough in advance so that there is time for a reply. It should not say, "We are coming on Saturday," but rather, "If you and John are free Saturday morning about 10:00, may we drop by?"

When you are on the receiving end of an unannounced visit, you have every right to carry on with any previous plans you might have made. Other than the normal requirement of being courteous to *any* visitor, you have no actual obligation to an unannounced visitor. If Aunt Mary arrives unexpectedly from 300 miles away and you had been planning to go to a church supper, simply suggest that she go along with you. If, however, you are expected at the Petersons' for bridge, have Aunt Mary make herself at home until your return. If possible, find something in the refrigerator or the cupboard that will serve as a snack or light meal. But you need not make yourself late for your appointment by taking the time to prepare a full dinner.

When the visitor is a friend or acquaintance from nearby, you can merely say, "Gee, I'm terribly sorry, but we were just leaving for the theater. Could we visit another time?" *And make the future date definite then and there.* "Another time" left at that means little, but a firm invitation proves that you really look forward to a visit—but at a more convenient moment.

In etiquette, as in most other things, there are exceptions. Casual drop-ins at Christmas and Thanksgiving are common in many parts of the country, when visitors bearing gifts and good cheer are expected. Even then, it's a good idea to call first before you drop by.

MEALTIME DROP-INS

If by chance you are just about to start your dinner when friends drop in, the polite response is to try to make the meal stretch to include them. If they say, "Oh, no, thank you—we've just eaten," pull up a chair for them, offer them a cup of coffee or a cold drink, and ask their forgiveness while you finish your meal. No one who drops in unannounced can expect you to let your meal get cold while you visit or magically produce two more portions. If the meal cannot possibly feed an extra person or two, explain that you were about to eat and ask if they could stop by later.

The same holds true when visitors arrive unexpectedly and you already have invited guests. You may ask them to join you if you are just sitting and chatting, but if you have invited a couple to play bridge, for example, your obligation is to them. Continue the game, asking the newcomers if they would like to watch. Only if the invited guests insist on stopping the game should you do so.

CHAPTER 25

TIPS ON TOASTS

The custom of toasting goes back almost as far as history itself. Ancient warriors drank to their pagan gods, Greeks and Romans drank to more gods, and early Norsemen drank to each other. Almost every culture practiced toasting in some form, and the custom gradually evolved into today's toasts to love, friendship, health, wealth, and happiness.

One story has it that the term itself originated in England in the seventeenth century, when it was customary to float a bit of toast on a drink. A well-known belle of the day was in the public baths (in Bath, where then, as now, the waters were considered salubrious). Her lover scooped up a little of the bath water, added the customary toast, and, having drunk to her health, offered the glass to a friend. The friend commented that he didn't really want the water but he'd enjoy the toast.

At one time or another, it is likely that you will be called upon to propose a toast. It is intimidating enough to get up in front of a group and make a prepared toast; but the thought of being called upon to make an impromptu one can be terrifying. The best solution? Speak from the heart—say exactly what you feel. The heartfelt toast doesn't have to be long, and if you do panic when called on unexpectedly, you can get away with something as brief as "To Ken, God bless him," or "To Greta—a wonderful friend for many years."

But if you want to say something a tad more eloquent or profound, dip into your bag of memories and share a reminiscence. Or tell a relevant anecdote. Or shower the honoree with (sincere) praise. A touch of humor is rarely out of place. The toast should always, however, be in keeping with the occasion and in good taste.

THE WAY IT WORKS

At a dinner party, it is the host or hostess's prerogative to offer the first toast. If none is offered, a guest may certainly propose a toast to the hosts. If one of the hosts has given the first toast, a guest may propose a second one. At informal dinners anyone may propose a toast as soon as wine or champagne is served. The toasters need not drain their glasses. A small sip each time allows one to drink numerous toasts from one serving.

Years ago you could toast only with an alcoholic beverage, but today you can use whatever liquid is available. Nondrinkers should raise their water goblet or glass of soda. Whether you drink or not, you must rise and join in the spirit at least—it is extremely discourteous to remain seated.

On ceremonial occasions there is generally a toastmaster, and if not, the chairman of the committee or the president of the organization proposes the necessary toasts at the end of the meal, and before any speeches.

REPLYING TO A TOAST

The person being toasted does not rise or drink the toast. Instead the honoree rises and drinks to his or her toasters in return, either saying, "Thank you," or proposing his own toast to them. Or, the reply to a toast may simply be a smile and a nod in the direction of the speaker or a raise of the glass toward the speaker in a gesture of "Thanks, and here's to you, too," after the toast has been completed.

SOME SAMPLE TOASTS

The following toasts are intended to give you some ideas for various occasions. They provide a framework in which to express your own feelings.

TOAST TO A RETIRING EMPLOYEE OR A MEMBER OF THE FIRM

"It is often said that nobody is indispensable, and that may sometimes be true. But for all of us there will never be anyone who can replace Joe. Although we will miss him greatly, we know how much he is looking forward to his retirement, and we wish him all the happiness he so richly deserves in the years to come."

Toast to a Guest of Honor at a Testimonial Dinner

"We are gathered here tonight to honor a woman who has given unselfishly of her time and effort to make this campaign so successful. Without the enthusiasm and leadership that Jane Wilson has shown all through these past months, we could never have reached our goal. Please join me in drinking a toast to the woman who, more than anyone else, is responsible for making it possible to see our dream of a new hospital wing finally come true."

Engagement-Party Toast

This is the conventional announcement made by the father of the bride-to-be at a party or dinner in celebration of the engagement of his daughter. After seeing that all glasses at the table are filled, the host rises, lifts his own glass, and says, "I propose we drink to the health of Mary and the man she has decided to add to our family. I would like to propose a toast to them both, wishing them a lifetime of happiness."

Everyone except the future bride and groom rises and drinks a little of whatever the beverage may be. The bride or the groom may stand and make a few remarks thanking the guests for their good wishes, expressing happiness with each other and with each other's new families.

Wedding-Celebration Toasts

Amend these toasts to fit the occasion when you are given the honor of making a toast at a wedding celebration, whether the rehearsal dinner or the reception.

A Bride's or Bridegroom's Father's Toast at the Rehearsal Dinner.
"I would like to ask you to join me in drinking a toast to two wonderful people without whom this wedding could never have been possible: Veronica's mother and father, Mr. and Mrs. Brown." And: "I don't need to tell you what a wonderful person Lynn is, but I do want to tell you how happy Brett's mother and I are to welcome her as our new daughter-in-law. To Lynn and Brett."

A Best Man's Toast to the Bridal Couple at the Wedding Reception.
"To Mary and John—may they always be as happy as they are today."

A Bridegroom's Toast to His Bride at the Wedding Reception.

"I'd like you all to join me in a toast to the woman who's just made me the happiest man in the world."

A Bride and Bridegroom's Toast to Their Parents and Guests.

"We would like you to join us in a toast to our wonderful parents who helped make this day possible. . . and now we toast all of you, our family and friends, with thanks for helping make this such a special time for us."

ANNIVERSARY TOAST

"Many of us who are here tonight can well remember that day 25 years ago when we drank a toast to the future happiness of Ann and Roger. It is more than obvious that our good wishes at that time have served them well, and therefore I would like to ask that all of you—old friends and new—rise and drink with me to another 25 years of the same love and happiness that Ann and Roger have already shared together."

TOASTS FOR ALL OCCASIONS

Following is a toast that can be added to the end of a few personal words or said on its own. It is one that has sent myriad travelers on their way, blessed countless couples, events, and special people and warmed the hearts of all present:

> *May you*
> *have warm words*
> *on a cold evening,*
> *A full moon*
> *on a dark night,*
> *And the road*
> *downhill*
> *all the way*
> *to your door.*

TOASTS IN OTHER LANGUAGES

Since the custom of toasting originated in Europe and is still more widely practiced there than here, well-traveled Americans are bringing home toasts from abroad. A knowledge of the most common of these can be very useful, but if you are not sure of the pronunciation use the equivalent English toast instead. The following examples all mean, translated, "To your health."

- FRENCH: *À votre santé.*

- SPANISH: *Salud.*

- GERMAN: *Prosit.*

- SWEDISH: *Sköal.* (This is often taken to mean that the toasters must empty their glasses, but that is not necessary in the United States.)

- YIDDISH: *L'Chayim.*

- IRISH: *Slàinte.*

- ITALIAN: *Salute.*

- RUSSIAN: *Na zdorovie.*

- POLISH: *Na zdrowie.*

CHAPTER 26

CATERERS AND TEMPORARY HELP

Even the most informal hostess sometimes needs help, whether a part-time helper to wash dishes or a full catering company to put on a dinner. Although the staff hired for the occasion may be professionals at what they do, you will still need to be around to supervise so that they are best able to do the job you hired them to do. Temporary help is generally employed for a social event to cook, serve, and/or clean up. It is up to the hostess to direct the help graciously while completing many of the other preparations, from setting the table and arranging flowers to making sure that the bar is stocked and that there is plenty of ice. Here are some tips on dealing with hired help for your social entertaining.

USING A CATERER

For a large party or a formal evening of entertaining, you may need to enlist professional workers to help you out. This could mean simply hiring a friend's college-age daughter to help. It may also mean using catering services and specialized employment agencies as resources for temporary help.

A catering service can provide any and all elements of the meal, from preparing a meal for the hostess to serve to doing all the cooking, serving, and cleaning up on the premises. A catering cook and staff should arrive early enough to learn the workings of the kitchen and have time for preparation of the meal, and a bartender should arrive to set up the bar well before guests are expected. If food is being prepared off the premises, it should be picked up or delivered early enough for the hostess to take care of whatever finishing touches are needed.

Caterers will also provide a complete wait staff, from bartenders to waiters and waitresses to a cleanup crew. Be sure to discuss what specific services will be required of your temporary help at the time the hiring arrangements are

made. You can use help in directing guests, taking coats, passing hors d'oeuvres, assisting the bartender, serving at the table, and cleaning up. Whatever
their duties will be, make sure they are all clearly spelled out in the contract.
Make sure the contract stipulates that servers and bartenders arrive before the
party starts to set up and familiarize themselves with the lay of the house.

Bartenders and waiters ordinarily do not leave until the last guest has been
ushered out, the last glass washed, and the last ashtray emptied. If, however, the
help has been hired on an hourly basis, the hostess may want to specify in
advance the hour that their duties will end. A cook generally leaves as soon as
the cooking utensils and dinner service have been washed and the kitchen
made immaculate.

Here are some tips on working with caterers:

- **GET A REFERRAL** Ask for names of recommended caterers from
  friends or coworkers. If you attend a party where the catering is outstanding,
  get the caterer's card for future reference.
- **FIND OUT WHAT IS INCLUDED** Does the caterer design centerpieces and, if so, does he offer choices? Does the caterer provide china, silverware, and glasses? Are gratuities included in the total price? What are over-
  time costs?
- **GET IT IN WRITING** Make sure that everything you need done is
  detailed in the catering contract and is matched by a price. There is nothing
  worse than finding out after the fact that a service you assumed would be
  included in the overall bill is in fact an extra cost.
- **SAMPLE THE GOODS** Have potential caterers prepare two or three different items from their menu for you to taste test before you make a decision.
  Many caterers will prepare several courses at no cost.
- **STICK TO YOUR BUDGET** Don't be seduced into buying unnecessary
  services that you can do yourself.

COCKTAIL PARTY HELP

In deciding whether or not you need help for your cocktail party, you have two
main considerations: the number of guests you expect and how elaborate the
drinks and food you plan to serve are to be. If your party is small, guests can
make their own drinks and you can take care of the food. With a large number
of guests, however, you should consider hiring a bartender and/or serving help.

Unless the party fare is simple and easily set out before the guests arrive, the assistance of at least one helper is a good idea. Again, ask friends and acquaintances for the names of reliable help, or work through an agency that specializes in food and bartender service.

PAYING AND TIPPING

The method of paying temporary help varies in different localities and also depends on the policy of the agency. Some caterers include gratuities in their total price. Others send a bill indicating that you may add a tip. If your help has been hired from an employment agency or by you personally, simply pay them before they leave at the rate that you have agreed upon, adding the appropriate tip. The most important thing is to establish the method and amount of payment at the time the help is hired to avoid any embarrassment or unpleasantness later. If friends are helping you out, a small gift presented at the end of the evening is a nice token of appreciation.

CHAPTER 27

TO INVITE THE WEE ONES. . .
OR NOT

FOR THE HOST

Children and pets alter the tone of a party. Simply by their nature, kids and pets bring an informality to the party, and the hostess relinquishes some measure of control over the proceedings. If you as a host are inviting a couple to a dinner party but don't want their children to come, simply call and say, "Do you think you could get a sitter for Saturday night so that you and Jim could come to dinner?"

If children of friends are brought along on an adults-only visit, the gracious host invites them in. If the children are small, however, and you have valuable objects that could be damaged, you may ask them to wait a moment while you move the objects out of harm's way, mentioning that you weren't expecting the children. Spread paper and pencils on the kitchen table for the children to draw on, offer a snack, or find a program on television to keep the children occupied while you and your friends talk. Other than providing these diversions, you are not obligated to entertain the kids. It is the visiting parents' responsibility to be sure their children are well-behaved and occupied.

For those hosts who don't have young children living at home, it's a smart idea to childproof the premises before an expected visit from little ones. Remove anything breakable or sharp that is within easy reach. Shut the doors to rooms you consider off limits, and see that doors to cellar steps and low windows are tightly closed. Then, when safety precautions are taken care of, check the supply of recreational materials. A basket or sack of simple toys—coloring books, blocks, and comic books—or a sampling of children's videotapes goes a long way toward making the visit enjoyable for both parent and host. And a supply of cookies and milk or soft drinks fits the bill when the novelty of the toys wears off.

If you do include your friends' child on a dinner-party invitation, and that child proves to be ill-mannered—leans back, tilting your dining room chair, or neglects to remove his baseball cap—you have every right to correct him. But you should only reproach him for breaking house rules, not for displaying poor personal behavior. You can tell him that in your house you don't sing at the table or wear hats, but you should not correct his (admittedly poor) personal behavior. Any word about your expectations—"In our house, it's hats off!"—should be mentioned, preferably in private.

FOR THE GUESTS

The standard is: Unless your children—or pets—are specifically invited, leave them at home when you visit friends or attend a social gathering. Often, however, this is not always practical. It may be difficult for couples with young children, for example, or people who are new in town or who can't afford a baby-sitter, to get away. In those cases, it's perfectly all right to ask the host politely whether or not the kids can come, too.

If the answer is "yes," you as parents can ensure that your children will be welcome guests in many ways. Toddlers should not be taken on visits until they learn the meaning of "no." Don't let your child run around unsupervised or eat and drink wherever he wants—a host is perfectly within her rights to set limits and to verbally enforce them. Bring a bag of favorite toys to keep your child occupied. And, with the knowledge that young children generally have short attention spans, set a time limit for the visit. End the visit before that limit is reached.

If your child is a guest among adults at a dinner party, help her out ahead of time. Picky eaters should be taught that it is extremely rude to turn up their noses when offered something they don't like. Not only is it a display of bad manners, but it hurts the feelings of the host. Tell your child to say instead, "No, thank you," and teach your child how to say "I'd like a peanut butter and jelly sandwich, please" rather than shrugging or saying "I don't know" when offered a choice. Remind her of some of the things that comprise good table manners so that she can be just as proud as you are of her skills.

When it is not clear on the invitation whether your children are invited, ask. "Is this invitation adults only, or are the children included?" If this is too difficult, say, "We'd love to come, but I have to see if I can get a sitter." If your hosts intended for the kids to be included in the first place, they can then reply, "Oh, no, please bring the children."

HOSTING WITH CHILDREN

Many people who love party occasions aren't quite sure what to do with their own children when they entertain guests for dinner. If the kids are included, much of the focus will be on them; if they are young, you'll need to give them attention and at the same time be a thoughtful host to your guests.

If your guests are close family friends or relatives, then your children, if they are old enough, can be present at the dinner table and even help you prepare. If your children are young, you may want to hire a baby-sitter who can give them the attention they need, thus freeing you to be attentive to your guests yourself.

When small children—whether your own or your guests'—are included in your dinner plans, it's perfectly correct to let them be excused from the table earlier than the adults, if they please. Have some activities available to occupy them while the adults are still eating; a video is a smart, relatively sedate choice. Avoid any rowdy after-dinner games guaranteed to send your guests' children home all worked up.

ENTERTAINING AND PETS

Even if your pet is beautifully behaved, if it is not invited to a social event you should leave it at home. Unless you know that the people you are visiting loves animals, never just show up with a pet or ask whether you may bring a pet along on a visit. If they are not enthusiastic about your request, you have put them in a difficult position. If they make the suggestion on their own, naturally your pet may go. Be sure, before you accept on his behalf, that his behavior will be exemplary.

If, on the other hand, you are a guest in the home of people who own pets, how do you protest without appearing rude when the family cat jumps on your lap? As a guest, you need never be subjected to animals that are not perfectly behaved. Simply remain pleasant and ask that the animal be put in another room. Say, "I'm sorry, but cats [or dogs] really bother me—" or "My allergies have gotten so much worse—would you mind removing Tabby [or Fido] from the room until I leave?" A good host will automatically monitor the situation to make sure his cat or dog doesn't bother the guest. Although the host may tolerate a pet's jumping into laps, it is never right to assume that guests should as well.

CHAPTER 28

A GRAND FINALE

Ending a party graciously can be difficult when all concerned are having a wonderful time. If you're game and still energetic, it is never rude for the hosts to encourage their guests to stay a little longer.

When the last guest has gone, it's time to take off your shoes, put your feet up, and replay the occasion in your mind. This is a good opportunity to not only savor the good memories but to take stock, to discern what worked and what didn't. Was there plenty of food? Or too much? What was eaten and what was neglected? How on target were your calculations on the types and amounts of beverages offered? Did the food complement the drinks?

If your party was a dinner party, how well did you time the courses? Was hot food served hot? Was there enough for all to have seconds if they so wanted?

Did the mix of guests gel? Did your party hum with lively pockets of chatter? *Most important: Did your guests relax and enjoy themselves?*

For the host and hostess, this is the golden hour. The party was a success; guests have been sent away floating on a bubble of goodwill and contentment. As the architect of a wonderful time for all, you should give yourself a pat on the back—and start dreaming of your next fine occasion.

INDEX

accidents caused by guests, 138, 201–2
adult birthdays
    gifts, 85, 162
    parties, 85–86
age, and introductions, 141, 149–50, 151
Akikan (Islam birth ceremony), 95
alcohol. *See also* cocktails; wine
    at business lunch, 69
    and driving, 202
    guests mixing own drinks, 58
    inebriated guests, 78–79, 202–3
    nondrinkers, 139, 171
    and office parties, 78–79
    stocking the bar, 39
anniversary gifts, 83, 160–62
    traditional, 161
anniversary parties
    entertainment at, 82
    gifts, 83, 160–62
    invitations, 7
    photographs, 83
    planning, 81–82
    receiving line, 83
    refreshments, 82
    requesting no gifts, 160
    scheduling, 81
    seating arrangements, 83
    toasts, 82, 209
    who hosts, 81–82
aperitifs, 167
appetizers
    for cocktail parties, 40, 41
    eating etiquette, 195
apples, how to eat, 182
apricots, how to eat, 182, 185
Arab countries, customs in, 141
arrival time of guests, 111, 137
artichokes, how to eat, 182–83
asparagus, how to eat, 183

attire
    for Bar/Bat Mitzvahs, 88–89
    black tie, 10, 17
    for brunches, 101
    for confirmations, 87
    for First Communions, 86
    in foreign countries, 140–42
    formal, 10, 17
    for Hindu birth ceremony, 95
    informal, 17
    for Islam birth ceremony, 95
    for office parties, 77
    party, 16–17
    at private clubs, 64–65
    for quinceañera, 89
    semiformal, 17
    white tie, 10, 17
avocados, how to eat, 183

babies. *See* baby showers; newborns
baby showers
    for adopted babies, 85
    gifts, 162
    invitations, 84
    planning, 84
    for second babies, 85
    for single mothers, 85
    when to give, 83–84
bacon, how to eat, 183
bananas, how to eat, 183
barbecues, 105–6
Bar Mitzvah, 7, 87–88, 163
bartenders
    caterers as, 212
    friends as, 42
    host and hostess as, 40–41
    protocol for, 41–42
    temporary help as, 212–13
bathroom etiquette, 137